KEEP HOLDING ON

30 PROMISES FROM GOD YOU CAN CLING TO RIGHT NOW

Written by Katy McCown
Copyright © 2024 by Proverbs 31 Ministries
All Scripture quotations are English Standard Version (ESV) unless otherwise noted.

We must exchange whispers with God before shouts with the world.

LYSA TERKEURST

PAIR YOUR STUDY GUIDE WITH THE FIRST 5 MOBILE APP!

This study guide is designed to accompany your study of Scripture in the First 5 mobile app. You can use it as a standalone study or as an accompanying guide to the daily content within First 5.

First 5 is a free mobile app developed by Proverbs 31 Ministries to transform your daily time with God.

Go to the app store on your smartphone, download the First 5 app, and create a free account!

WWW.FIRST5.ORG

Welcome to our study on the promises of God.

Maybe you picked up this book because you've heard about the promises of God. You may even know they are available for you to cling to in your time of need. Maybe you're in need right now, feeling like everything you've tried to hold on to in life has crumbled in your hands, and you're reaching out for something — anything — sturdy and reliable.

If so, friend, I'm so glad you're joining me on this journey.

Sometimes, even if we're aware of God's promises to us in His Word, those promises feel like Christmas presents wrapped under the tree: We point to them with excitement, knowing something good is wrapped up inside. We glance toward them often with anticipation. We may even tell other people about the promises we have from the Lord. But all the while, the gifts remain wrapped, unopened.

And we all know a wrapped present isn't really what we want. We want what's inside! We would never leave a Christmas gift wrapped under the tree forever — because to truly enjoy the gift, we need to unwrap it, take it out of the box, and put it to use.

The promises of God are like those Christmas gifts. To truly cling to them, we have to do more than know they are there. We have to open God's Word, find His promises on the pages, and put them into practice in our day to day lives. That's what we'll do together over the next six weeks.

Each day, as you receive a promise from your loving Father, I pray that your spiritual grip will be strengthened so you can keep holding on to the great and precious promises God has given you to cling to *right now*.

Sincerely,
Katy

What Are the Promises of God?

In its most basic form, a promise is an assurance given by someone that they will do something or that something specific will happen. Promises bring expectation of action or anticipation of a certain result.

For the purposes of our study, the promises of God can be defined in this way: an assurance given by God in His Word. The pages of the Bible are rich with God's great and precious promises (2 Peter 1:3-4) of blessings He will surely bestow upon His people.[1] Included in these are God's promises of **peace, guidance, comfort, strength, security** and **hope**, which we will study together over the next six weeks.

In the ESV translation of the Bible, the word "promise" is used 66 times in 64 verses. These verses include promises between two or more people as well as promises between God and His people. Though we won't study all 64 of these verses in our six weeks together, today, as we begin our study, let's look at the *first* and *last* promises in Scripture.

The first promise in the Bible is found in Genesis, and it is viewed as the first announcement of the gospel. In this promise, God, speaking to Satan, said: *"I will put enmity between you and the woman, and between your offspring and her offspring; he shall bruise your head, and you shall bruise his heel"* (Genesis 3:15).

In response to humanity's sin, God gave subsequent consequences for disobeying Him, but He also promised His plan of redemption. The entire Bible reveals how God fulfilled this redemptive plan through His only Son, Jesus (John 3:16).

The last promise in Scripture comes in Revelation 22:20a, where God says, *"Surely I am coming soon."* Those who follow Jesus eagerly wait for the fulfillment of this promise that will bring God's redemptive plan to its eternal completion: Through faith in Jesus, we who were once God's enemies get to be God's children forever.

All of God's promises can be viewed through the lens of these two. Because of God's promise to redeem us from sin, we have peace, guidance, comfort and security. And when we cling to the promise that Jesus is coming soon, we find strength and hope for today.

HOW DO I KNOW I CAN TRUST THE PROMISES OF GOD?

Before we go any further in our study of God's promises, it is important to note that a promise is only as good as the one who makes it. Even the most well-meaning human beings can, at times, break a promise. At our core, we are imperfect and unable to control our circumstances. It hurts intensely when people make promises they don't even intend to keep — and it also hurts when we genuinely want to keep a promise but still let each other down.

You've probably felt the sting of an unkept promise. Because of that, you may be hesitant to trust God's promises — and if so, friend, you're not alone. Yet as we go through this study together, you will find that God has never made a promise He did not keep.

The Bible testifies that God is faithful and that His words come to pass (Joshua 23:14). God can be trusted because He is not only willing and able to accomplish what He promises (Romans 4:21), but He literally cannot do otherwise (Numbers 23:19; 2 Timothy 2:13). As Hebrews 6:18 says, *"It is impossible for God to lie."*

The chart below shows several promises from God, who He made the promises to, where you can find them in the Bible, and the places where Scripture records how God fulfilled His promise.

GOD'S PROMISE	WHO RECEIVED THE PROMISE	WHERE IT IS FULFILLED
"And I will make of you a great nation, and I will bless you and make your name great, so that you will be a blessing ... in you all the families of the earth shall be blessed" (Genesis 12:2-3).	Abram	Exodus 1:7; Joshua 21:44; Galatians 3:7-9
"... I will be with you, and you shall strike the Midianites as one man" (Judges 6:16).	Gideon	Judges 7
"... You shall cause this people to inherit the land that I swore to their fathers to give them" (Joshua 1:6).	Joshua	Joshua 12; Joshua 23:14; Ephesians 1:11
"Your throne shall be established forever" (2 Samuel 7:16b).	David	Luke 1:30-33
"And I will give you a new heart, and a new spirit I will put within you" (Ezekiel 36:26a). "And I will ask the Father, and he will give you another Helper, to be with you forever, even the Spirit of truth ..." (John 14:16-17)	God's people	Acts 2:2-4; Ephesians 1:13
"... do not be anxious how you are to speak or what you are to say, for what you are to say will be given to you in that hour" (Matthew 10:19).	Jesus' 12 disciples	Acts 4

These are just a few examples of God's promises and their fulfillment. In the weeks ahead, we will study passages from both the Old and New Testaments that deepen our understanding of God's promises in Scripture, the One who promised them, and how we can cling to them.

The more we know God, the more we will trust His promises. Take some time to review the promises in the chart above, and as you do, ask God to give you a heart that will trust Him to be faithful to His promises to you.

PROMISES OF GOD
In the Old Testament and the New Testament

God made many promises in the Old Testament; however, they are not always articulated with the word "promise." The Hebrew words most frequently used in connection with God's promises are *dābhār*, which means "speaking" or "speech," and *āmar*, which means "to say."[1]

God's promises in the Old Testament often take the form of covenants with a specific person or people. The formal definition of a "covenant" is "an arrangement between two parties involving mutual obligations." In the biblical sense, it is "the arrangement that established the relationship between God and his people, expressed in grace first with Israel and then with the church."[2] The covenant theme is a centerpiece of the Bible, so much so that the Old and New Testaments of the Bible have also been called the old covenant and new covenant.[3]

The Old Testament records covenants God made with:

- Adam (Genesis 1:26-30, Genesis 2:16-17).
- Noah (Genesis 8:21-22; Genesis 9:1-17).
- Abraham (Genesis 12; Genesis 15; Genesis 17).
- Moses and the Israelites (Exodus 19:1-6; Exodus 24).
- David (2 Samuel 7).

In scriptures like Jeremiah 31:31-34 and Ezekiel 36:25-28, we also see promises that a totally new covenant of the heart was coming. In the New Testament, through Jesus, God made this new covenant that allows all people to access forgiveness of sins and the free gift of salvation through faith in Christ (Matthew 5:17; Ephesians 2:8-9). New Testament promises are therefore not separate or isolated from the promises made in the Old Testament, but instead they serve as unified promises that are ultimately fulfilled in Jesus.[4]

- New Testament promises reference Jesus as the ultimate fulfillment of God's promises to **Abraham** concerning the heir he would receive (Romans 4:13-16; Galatians 3:16-29).
- New Testament promises point to Jesus, the Messiah, as the promised seed of **David** who will reign forever (Acts 13:22-23; Romans 1:1-3).
- The New Testament book of Hebrews also references God's promises to make His people into a **nation** in a God-given **land** in the Old Testament, filling these promises with new spiritual and eternal significance in light of Jesus (Hebrews 4:8-9; Hebrews 6:15-18; Hebrews 11:8-10).

Because *"all the promises of God find their Yes in him [Jesus]"* (2 Corinthians 1:20a), Christians today are heirs of the new covenant, and we also interpret and apply Old Testament promises in light of the life, death, burial and resurrection of Christ.

HOW DO I KNOW WHICH OF GOD'S PROMISES ARE FOR ME?

The Bible contains a few different types of **proverbs**, **promises** and **principles**, and it's important to know the differences between these as we faithfully seek to apply the Word of God to our lives.

Some of God's promises are *specific*, intended for a particular person or situation. Other promises are *timeless* and applicable to God's people in the past, present and future. Along with these specific and timeless promises, God also gives us general *principles* or truths we can take from Scripture and apply to our lives today. Let's look at each of these in more detail:

PROVERBS

Proverbs in Scripture are primarily principles of wisdom, not promises. They give us guidance for wise, righteous living, and they are rich with fundamental truths about God, often stating a supposed or reasonable outcome for a godly way of life. But for the most part, they do not guarantee that outcome in all situations. For instance, *"a slack hand causes poverty, but the hand of the diligent makes rich"* (Proverbs 10:4); however, this is not a guarantee that all poverty is caused by lack of diligence or that all diligent people will definitely be rich. Pastor John Piper describes it like this: "Proverbs, by their very nature, are generalizations about the way life usually is rather than promises about the way it will have to be all the time."[1]

PROMISES: SPECIFIC OR TIMELESS?

While proverbs often focus on what is ideal or probable rather than what is absolute, God's promises are absolutely guaranteed 100% of the time. Some of God's specific promises have already come true in biblical history, whereas other promises are timelessly true for generations of His people, including us today. To help us differentiate between specific promises and timeless promises in Scripture, here are four questions we can ask when we approach a passage:

1. What is the context of the promise?
2. Is the promise directed toward a specific person or group of people?

3. Is the promise connected to a specific time or event in history?
4. If this is a specific promise God made to a person/people in the past, what principles can I learn from it today?

For an example, we can look at Jeremiah 29:11: *"For I know the plans I have for you, declares the LORD, plans for welfare and not for evil, to give you a future and a hope."*

To consider the context of the promise, we need to read the entire chapter of Jeremiah 29. According to Jeremiah 29:1, *"These are the words of the letter that Jeremiah the prophet sent from Jerusalem to the surviving elders of the exiles, and to the priests, the prophets, and all the people, whom Nebuchadnezzar had taken into exile from Jerusalem to Babylon."*

Here we see the answer to question No. 1: The specific recipients of the Jeremiah 29:11 promise were the surviving elders of the exiles, the priests, prophets and all the people of Israel who had been taken into exile.

To answer the second and third questions, we can read Jeremiah 29:10: *"For thus says the LORD: When seventy years are completed for Babylon, I will visit you, and I will fulfill to you my promise and bring you back to this place."*

Now that we've determined this was a specific promise God made to bring Israel back from exile in the past, we can look for principles that may still apply to God's people today even though we are not Israelites exiled in Babylon. Woven into this passage are the fundamental truths that God is good, that He pursues His people in spite of their disobedience, and that His plan for His people remains even when they face consequences of sinful choices.

HOLDING ON TO WHAT'S PROMISED

So, once we identify a promise from God that applies to us, what do we actually do with it? The Bible shows us many examples of how God's people clung to His promises.

For instance, let's look at Jacob, the son of Isaac, the promised son of Abraham and Sarah (Genesis 25:19-27). In his youth, Jacob stole the blessing of his older brother, Esau, and in retaliation, Esau planned to kill Jacob. Jacob fled for the land of Paddan-aram, and while there, he married, had children and grew in wealth (Genesis 27-30).

In Genesis 32, Jacob was returning to his homeland, but he feared backlash from Esau — so much so that he made a plan in case Esau attacked him. In this moment, he clung to the promises God had made to his family. He told God, **"But you said,** *'I will surely do you good, and make your offspring as the sand of the sea, which cannot be numbered for multitude'"* (Genesis 32:12, emphasis added). Jacob's words were confident: *You said.* He remembered what God had promised him and repeated it in his time of need.

This was a promise and not simply a principle. Jacob's family, the nation of Israel, became a great multitude as promised. We pray this study guide will give you promises to remember and repeat just as Jacob did.

MORE EXAMPLES OF
Promises and Principles

SCRIPTURE	SPECIFIC PROMISE FOR A PERSON/PEOPLE IN THE PAST	TIMELESS PROMISE TO ALL GOD'S PEOPLE	PRINCIPLE FOR EVERYONE
Genesis 17:15-19	Old, barren Sarah would bear a child.		God can do miracles.
Jeremiah 29:11	God would bring Israel from exile.		God cares about His people and delivers them.
Ezekiel 36:26-27		God will put His Spirit in His people and will give us hearts of flesh.	God is intimate and cares about our hearts.
Isaiah 25:8		God will swallow up death forever for His people.	God is opposed to evil.
Proverbs 10:4			Generally, being lazy doesn't produce financial stability.
Proverbs 10:3			Generally, God provides humankind with food, especially those who are in His service.
Philippians 4:13			Christians can have joy even in suffering and can be useful for God's Kingdom even in situations as dire as being in prison, like Paul was when he wrote this.

The Promise of Sin Versus the Better Promises of God

The Bible gives us many promises from God, and we often find blessings that come with them. However, we cannot study this subject without also discussing another kind of promise: When we choose to disobey God, we forfeit His good, eternal promises for the worldly promises of sin.

These opposing promises have been present from the beginning. Long ago, God promised humans dominion over the earth and provision of everything they could ever need to thrive. He also promised the blessings of fruitfulness and unbroken fellowship with Him in the goodness of His perfect creation (Genesis 1:26-31).

Yet in the midst of all of God's promises, the serpent, Satan, appeared and made promises of his own. Satan promised Eve she wouldn't die, then promised that her eyes would be opened, if she ate the fruit God had forbidden (Genesis 3:4-5). Both were lies — false promises he could never fulfill. But she believed him … and suffered the consequences of the promises she believed.

The truth is that sin promises the wrath of God (Romans 2:8). Sin promises hopelessness (Ephesians 2:12). Sin promises to darken our understanding and alienate us from God and His promises (Ephesians 4:18).

When we entertain sin, we're promised we will destroy each other (Galatians 5:15). Sin will make us think we're free but will actually make us slaves to corruption (2 Peter 2:19). Ultimately, *"the wages of sin is death"* (Romans 6:23).

When we're faced with the choice of indulging in our sin nature or living by the Holy Spirit and obeying God, let's remember what sin really promises, and let's choose the better promises of our Savior.

Many promises in Scripture are tied to our participation. Oftentimes receiving a promise calls for a choice of obedience to our Lord. As we study the promises of God, be on the lookout for a green circle (●) — each time you see it, you'll know there is a promise that requires our participation.

11

What You Have To Look Forward to in This Guide

DAILY TEACHINGS AND REFLECTION QUESTIONS

Each week of this study includes daily teachings on five promises of God. We will unwrap the promises together and learn how to apply them in our daily lives. You'll also find daily questions to guide your personal study.

WEEKEND REFLECTIONS AND PRAYING THE PROMISES

Each weekend, we will summarize some important ideas we've learned throughout the week and will close with a prayer written from the words of a psalm or another passage of Scripture that reflects the promise we've studied that week.

CLINGING TO THE PROMISES

As you work through this study, you will also find pages entitled "Clinging to the Promises." These pages are designed to give you additional promises from God that you can apply directly to situations you're facing today, along with prompts to help you cling to the promises in prayer.

MAJOR MOMENTS

WEEK 1:
Promise of Peace

DAY 1 (Judges 6:1-27)
God will bring peace when it seems impossible.

DAY 2 (Isaiah 9:1-7)
God's peace will make you whole.

DAY 3 (John 14:25-31)
God's peace will give you confidence and courage.

DAY 4 (Isaiah 26)
God will keep you in perfect peace.

DAY 5 (Philippians 4:1-9)
God will guard your heart and mind against anxiety.

WEEK 2
Promise of Guidance

DAY 6 (Genesis 12:1-9)
God will lead you one faithful step at a time.

DAY 7 (Exodus 14)
God will remind you that He made a way when it seemed like there was no way.

DAY 8 (John 8:12-30)
God will light the way so you do not stumble.

DAY 9 (John 16:5-15)
God will guide you when the road ahead feels uncertain.

DAY 10 (James 1)
God will give you wisdom when you need it.

WEEK 3
Promise of Comfort

DAY 11 (Genesis 16)
God will always see you.

DAY 12 (Ezekiel 34:11-24)
God will diligently care for you.

DAY 13 (John 10:1-18)
God will comfort you with His voice.

DAY 14 (1 Peter 5:1-11)
God will carry all of your burdens and worries.

DAY 15 (2 Corinthians 1:1-11)
God will comfort you in your troubles.

WEEK 4:
Promise of Strength

DAY 16 (Genesis 17:1-21)
God will never fail you.

DAY 17 (Isaiah 41:1-20)
God will hold you up when you are afraid.

DAY 18 (John 6:22-58)
God will sustain you.

DAY 19 (2 Corinthians 12:1-10)
God will be your strength when you are weak.

DAY 20 (Ephesians 6:10-20)
God will give you His strength so you can stand.

WEEK 5:
Promise of Security

DAY 21 (2 Samuel 22)
God will be your place of safety.

DAY 22 (Isaiah 27:1-6)
God will keep watch over you and your future.

DAY 23 (John 15:1-17)
God will remain in you.

DAY 24 (2 Peter 1:1-11)
God will give you everything you need.

DAY 25 (Hebrews 13:1-18)
God will never leave you.

WEEK 6:
Promise of Hope

DAY 26 (Hebrews 10:19-39)
God will be faithful.

DAY 27 (Romans 8:18-30)
God will work all things for good.

DAY 28 (Matthew 11:25-30)
God will give you rest when you are weary and burdened.

DAY 29 (John 11:17-44)
God will raise you up when life feels hopeless.

DAY 30 (Revelation 21:1-8)
God will wipe away every tear.

WEEK ONE

PROMISE OF PEACE

DAY 1

JUDGES 6:1-27: God will bring peace when it seems impossible.

Today's reading reveals circumstances that would make peace seem impossible.

In fact, the general context of the Old Testament book of Judges is one of war, chaos and lawlessness during an era when Israel had no king. Again and again, God's people disobeyed Him and suffered the consequences of that disobedience as they were afflicted by various enemies (Judges 2:18-19). Eventually, the Israelites were hiding in caves and in the mountains for fear of oppression from the Midianites (Judges 6:1-6).

Read Judges 6:3-6, and record some of the details of the circumstances in Israel.

Where was Gideon and what was he doing when *"the angel of the LORD"* met him at Ophrah (Judges 6:11-12)?

Typically, people would have beaten out wheat on a threshing floor; however, Gideon was in a winepress, a sunken area used for the grape harvest. Gideon's actions reflected his fear of the Midianites as he sought to hide and disguise his activity.[1]

According to Judges 6:14-16, what did God send Gideon to do, and what did He promise?

In the wake of what felt like an impossible task, Gideon asked for a sign. Upon receiving the sign, Gideon built an altar and called it *yhwh shalom*, "The LORD Is Peace" (Judges 6:24).

"The LORD Is Peace" was not only a response to God's promise to bring peace to Israel and rescue them from the hand of Midian but more directly a response to the reality that Gideon had seen God (or *"the angel of the LORD"*) face to face and lived (Judges 6:22-23).

In Exodus 33:20, God said it was impossible for sinful man to come face to face with Him, the holy God, and live. Yet God made it possible for Gideon to experience something of His heavenly presence, and then He gave another promise: *"Peace be to you. Do not fear; you shall not die"* (Judges 6:23).

> Now let's put into practice what we learned about discerning God's promises back on pages 8-9 of this guide. In what ways were God's promises in Judges 6 *specifically* addressed to Gideon? What principles still apply to our lives today?

God fulfilled His promise to Gideon and to Israel. In a way only He could, God used Gideon to defeat Midian and save His people (Judges 7). And God also made a way for us to have eternal peace with Him: Through the sacrificial death of His one and only Son, Jesus, God made peace with all who trust in Him (Romans 5:1-2; Romans 5:10-11). As God promised Gideon, *"Peace ... you shall not die"* (Judges 6:23), He promises us that *"whoever believes in [Jesus] should not perish but have eternal life"* (John 3:16).

> Have you ever felt like it was impossible for you to draw near to God and have peace with Him? How do Judges 6:23 and John 3:16 encourage you, even if you are not experiencing peaceful circumstances right now?

God revealed Himself to Gideon, and reveals Himself to us, as the God of peace.

If your circumstances seem insurmountable …
If you feel far away from God …
If you feel afraid or incapable or ill-equipped …

You can cling to God today and trust that because of the Lord of peace, you can have *"peace at all times"* (2 Thessalonians 3:16), including when it seems impossible.

DAY 2
ISAIAH 9:1-7: God's peace will make you whole.

Yesterday we learned about the God of peace and how He defeated Midian, one of Israel's enemies (Judges 6-7). Today's reading recalls that defeat (Isaiah 9:4). Five hundred years later, it still lingered in the memory of the prophet Isaiah and the nation of Israel as one of the most outstanding examples of God's ability to bring deliverance against overwhelming odds.[1]

At the time Isaiah was prophesying, Israel faced a coming Assyrian invasion and the exile that would follow (Isaiah 8). The outlook was bleak, but in the midst of the darkness of their circumstances, God revealed the coming Light (Isaiah 9:2).

Years later, a priest named Zechariah would recall Isaiah's words when he prophesied of the birth of Jesus, the Messiah, *"because of the tender mercy of our God, whereby the sunrise shall visit us from on high to give light to those who sit in darkness and in the shadow of death ..."* (Luke 1:78-79).

> These verses also expand on the purpose of the Light. What does Luke 1:79 say the Light will do for our feet?

Just as Zechariah's prophecy of the coming Messiah promised peace, Isaiah's prophecy did too.

> List the four names given to the Messiah in Isaiah 9:6:

During the time of Isaiah's prophecy, the birth of an heir to the throne would have been a momentous occasion. The new king ascending to the throne would have taken a title or name for himself to embody his best qualities, accomplishments or attributes.[2] As we study the promise of God's peace, we will focus on how Isaiah 9:6 names Jesus the *"Prince of Peace."* The word translated *"peace"* comes from a Hebrew word (shalom) that means "to be whole, complete."[3]

What does Isaiah 9:7 say about how long the peace of Jesus will last?

As a note, words like *"forevermore"* (v. 7) are ones we can pay attention to as we discern the promises of God that apply to us today; this language indicates a timeless promise!

A few chapters later, Isaiah describes Jesus' reign of peace with a beautiful scene where natural enemies such as wolves and lambs dwell in harmony together (Isaiah 11:6-7). In Jesus' eternal Kingdom, there will be no fear of harm or hurt, *"for the earth shall be full of the knowledge of the L*ORD*"* (Isaiah 11:9).

While we wait for the complete fulfillment of Jesus' reign of peace in eternity, we can experience the peace that comes from the saving knowledge of God through Christ today. What does Colossians 1:19-20 say Jesus is doing with *"all things, whether on earth or in heaven"*?

What would it take for you to feel like you have peace, wholeness and completeness in your life?

To be whole, we first have to know what is missing. By calling Jesus the Prince of Peace, Isaiah drilled down to the true missing piece in our lives: We must allow the shalom, the peace, the *wholeness*, found in Jesus to shape our perspective of the circumstances that surround us. As our knowledge of the Prince of Peace increases, so also will our peace increase.

Biblical Word Study: "Peace"

	WORD USED FOR "PEACE"	DEFINITION	KEY PASSAGES
Old Testament	Šālôm (Hebrew)	completeness, soundness, welfare[1]	Genesis 15:15 Joshua 9:15 Isaiah 54:10 Isaiah 59:8
New Testament	Eirēnē (Greek)	the tranquil state of a soul assured of salvation through Christ, and so fearing nothing from God and content with one's earthly lot[2]	Romans 8:6 2 Peter 3:14 John 16:33 Philippians 4:7

DAY 3

JOHN 14:25-31: God's peace will give you confidence and courage.

Jesus gave His disciples the words in John 14 at a time when they were distressed. Fast-forwarding several centuries after yesterday's reading in the book of Isaiah, the events of today's reading took place after the Last Supper and before the crucifixion of Jesus. Jesus had just told His followers that some of them would betray Him (John 13:26; John 13:38) and that He was going away (John 14:1-7) — and they were clearly confused. Worried. Afraid.

Jesus even began the chapter with the words, *"Let not your hearts be troubled"* (John 14:1) because while He knew His departure would be something to celebrate, the news struck fear and concern in the hearts of His disciples (John 14:5). And in response to their distress, Jesus gave them a promise.

> According to John 14:27, what promise did Jesus give His disciples?

> What response did Jesus ask for in light of His promise?

Jesus' peace gives us confidence to cling to Him and courage to be changed by Him

First, the peace Jesus gives us is personal. Jesus said, **"My** *peace I give to you"* (John 14:27, emphasis added).

> What do Ephesians 2:14 and Ephesians 2:17 say about Jesus' peace? Where does it come from?

21

The peace Jesus gives us doesn't depend on anyone or anything else. Jesus doesn't have to borrow peace from someone or somewhere in order to give it to His disciples. This personal peace also points us to the fact that Jesus is not distant or absent. He is aware of and attentive to our circumstances, always standing ready to give us His peace.

Second, the peace Jesus gives us is complete. The Greek word translated "*peace*" in John 14:27 is *eirēnēn*. D.A. Carson describes this as peace that "secures composure in the midst of trouble, and dissolves fear."[1] It's so much more than the waves of life being calmed for a moment. It's a wholeness that holds us together even in the midst of suffering and disappointment.

Third, the peace Jesus gives us cannot be found anywhere else. Jesus told His disciples He gives peace *"not as the world gives"* (John 14:27). Two chapters later, in John 16, Jesus elaborated on what His disciples could expect from the world: trouble, tribulation, distress and frustration (John 16:33). The world will never satisfy our souls with peace. The Old Testament prophet Jeremiah also spoke of worldly liars who would say, *"'Peace, peace,' when there is no peace"* (Jeremiah 6:14). However, Jesus contrasted what the world gives with the promise of His perfect peace.

Jesus' peace gives us confidence and courage in the face of trials. His peace encourages us and equips us to live with unshakable faith.

> Where do you most need the peace of Christ in your life right now?

> Review the distinctions of the peace Jesus promises us. In your own words, ask Jesus for His peace, and ask Him to help you receive it with assurance.

DAY 4

ISAIAH 26: God will keep you in perfect peace.

Isaiah 26:1 opens with the words, "*In that day this song will be sung ...*" signaling a future time that had yet to be realized for Isaiah's original Israelite audience.

Scholars differ on whether they believe Isaiah's prophecy points to the final events of history or to events that were in the near future of the prophet at the time. The best answer might actually be both: Old Testament prophecies often include a short-term and long-term fulfillment, which is how this chapter gives us timeless promises of peace we can still cling to today.

Twice in this chapter, in the midst of images of chaos and judgment for the unrighteous, Isaiah tells us about the peace God's children can expect.

First, Isaiah 26:3 says, "*You [God] keep him in perfect peace whose mind is stayed on you, because he trusts in you.*" The perfect peace Isaiah wrote about is an all-embracing peace.[1] It describes an overall mindset and approach to life from the perspective of peace. But this promise also requires action from us.

> Who specifically does this verse say God keeps in perfect peace?

The Amplified Bible expands on the participation required for this perfect peace. It says, "*You will keep in perfect and constant peace the one whose mind is steadfast [that is, committed and focused on You—in both inclination and character], Because he trusts and takes refuge in You [with hope and confident expectation]*" (Isaiah 26:3).

Later in this chapter, Isaiah explains more about how to have a mind committed to and focused on the Lord:

1. To focus our minds on God, we must commit to walk the path of righteousness and obedience to God (Isaiah 26:7). The words of verse 7 show that God goes ahead of His people and smooths out their path.
2. Isaiah also describes the obedient people of God as waiting expectantly for Him and desiring for His name to be known and glorified (Isaiah 26:8-9).

At First 5, we primarily cite scriptures from the ESV Bible, but we've also cited the Amplified Bible a few times throughout this study. The AMP Bible was published in 1965 and "uses synonyms and definitions to explain and expand the meaning of words ... placing amplification in parentheses, brackets, and after keywords." According to the publisher, these amplifications aim "to reveal a word's intensity or power along with the shades of meaning in the Hebrew, Aramaic, or Greek."[2] We pray that reading scriptures in a few different translations helps you gain a rich understanding of God's Word.

In your quest for peace, have you included obedience to God and expectant waiting on Him? Which one might you need to do more of?

When our minds are focused on God and our hearts trust in Him, we cooperate with the peace God desires to give His children. However, at the same time as He invites our participation, peace from God ultimately does not depend on what we can do but on what He can do.

Look up the scriptures below, and record what they say about our works and God's grace.

EPHESIANS 2:8-9:

2 TIMOTHY 1:9:

TITUS 3:5:

As we walk the paths of righteousness established by the Lord, He promises to keep us in perfect peace. The Lord brings us into peace. The Lord keeps us there. Isaiah 26:12 speaks of how God *"will ordain peace"* for His people. To ordain or establish peace means to "put something in place" or to "appoint someone to experience."[3] As God's children, we are God-appointed to experience God's peace.

Peace has been promised to us. Peace has been appointed for us. Today, let's commit our minds to God and cling to His promise of peace.

DAY 5

PHILIPPIANS 4:1-9: God will guard your heart and mind against anxiety.

In Philippians 4, the Apostle Paul was writing to encourage humility and harmony among followers of Jesus in a place called Philippi, first by telling them to seek godly peace in their relationships (Philippians 4:2-3) and then to seek godly peace in their own hearts. Paul described the peace of God in two ways:

1. It *"surpasses all understanding"* (Philippians 4:7).
2. It *"will guard your hearts and your minds in Christ Jesus"* (Philippians 4:7).

"Surpass[ing] all understanding" means the peace of God is far greater than human reasoning can comprehend.

> Have you ever heard someone try to explain a personal experience of the peace of God? What words did they use?

> Why do you think it's actually **good** that we can't fully comprehend or explain God's peace? (What might it suggest about God's limitlessness and our limits?)

The peace of God also guards us against anxiety. The Greek verb translated *"guard"* in Philippians 4:7 is *phroureō*, which reflects the idea of protection by a military guard. It evokes the visual of a guard who patrols the heart like a soldier mounted on horseback, whose job is to keep watch. It's the scene of being surrounded — not by an enemy poised for attack but by the incomprehensible blessings of God.[1]

> Consider something you are anxious about right now. In light of this promise, how does envisioning yourself surrounded by and guarded by God's peace change your heart?

At this point, you might be thinking: This peace sounds great ... but how do we actually get it? Well, verse 7 starts with the word *"and"* for a reason — it's connected to verse 6, where Paul carves a path to lead us to the promise of God's peace.

What does Philippians 4:6 describe as the path to peace?

Paul used three near-synonyms here: *"prayer," "supplication"* and *"requests."* According to commentators, the first word Paul used for "prayer" would often point to intercession for others.[2] Intercession is the practice of praying on behalf of someone.

How could praying for someone today help you release your anxiety and receive God's peace?

Paul used the word *"supplication,"* also sometimes translated "petition," to describe "an urgent request to meet a need, exclusively addressed to God."[3] Paul knew well the effectiveness of petitions presented before God. He used the same word to describe his prayer for the Philippians (Philippians 1:3-4) as well as their prayers for him (Philippians 1:19).

So often we may be inclined to turn to someone or something else in times of urgent need, but the peace of God that surpasses all understanding is accessed through prayer and supplication exclusively addressed to God.

Finally, the word *"requests"* in Philippians 4:6 includes the naming of specific items. This isn't a vague or broad kind of prayer; instead it's the intimacy of sharing specific burdens of our hearts with our God of peace, who desires to guard our hearts and minds.

What specific requests do you need to bring to God in prayer today?

As Paul taught about the path to peace through prayer, he also instructed Christians to pray *"with thanksgiving"* (v. 6). Today, let's give thanks for God's promise of peace.

WEEKEND REFLECTION
WEEK 1

This week we've walked a path lined with the stepping stones to peace. We've learned about where peace is possible and how it's possible. Most importantly, we've learned our peace is tied directly to Jesus.

As we conclude this week, let's remember that Jesus is the place where we find confidence to know God's will and access to enjoy His fellowship and intimacy. When we walk with Him step by step, we can be assured that the peace of God will rule in our hearts — which is indeed the way we are called to live (Colossians 3:15).

PRAYING THE PROMISES (PSALM 119:165)
Dear God, today I give thanks for the promise of perfect peace You give to Your people. I want the peace of Christ to rule in my heart. Show me the places where I seek peace apart from the company of Christ, and give me the courage to instead lean on You alone and to love Your law like Psalm 119:165 says. Thank You for the abundant peace that belongs to Your children. In Jesus' name, amen.

NOTES

NOTES

CLINGING TO GOD'S PROMISES WHEN YOU FACE TEMPTATION TO SIN

Dear God, today I am facing temptation in these areas of my life:

To cling to Your promises, I will remember Your Word says:

"No temptation has overtaken you that is not common to man. God is faithful, and he will not let you be tempted beyond your ability, but with the temptation he will also provide the way of escape, that you may be able to endure it" *(1 Corinthians 10:13).*

"... Pray that you may not enter into temptation" *(Luke 22:40).*

"If we confess our sins, he is faithful and just to forgive us our sins and to cleanse us from all unrighteousness" *(1 John 1:9).*

"For as high as the heavens are above the earth, so great is his steadfast love toward those who fear him; as far as the east is from the west, so far does he remove our transgressions from us" *(Psalm 103:11-12).*

In Jesus' name, amen.

WEEK TWO

PROMISE OF GUIDANCE

DAY 6

GENESIS 12:1-9: God will lead you one faithful step at a time.

One of the most famous promises in the Bible is the Abrahamic covenant in the book of Genesis. It's hard to overstate how important this promise was and is for God's people and how often it's referenced in Scripture (e.g., Deuteronomy 29:13; Micah 7:20; Acts 3:25; Hebrews 6:13-15). So let's apply to this covenant some of the questions we learned from the introduction of our study (page 8).

According to Genesis 12:1-3, what promise did God make?

To whom did God make the promise?

Which parts of the promise were specific to one person, and which parts are more timeless or applicable to others?

God's promise to guide Abram was a specific promise to him and his family, who would become the nation of Israel. In one sense, this promise is not for every person in the world. We are not each called to leave our countries so that our families will become mighty nations. But there is an aspect of this promise that *does* apply to us.

Read Galatians 3:7-9. Who are the children of Abraham today, and what do we receive?

We can also draw principles, or foundational truths, from God's guidance of Abram that we can apply to our lives today:

First, God's guidance to him didn't include many details. God simply said, *"Go ... to the land that I will show you"* (Genesis 12:1).

Abram had to leave everything that was familiar and comfortable to follow God into the unknown (Genesis 12:4-5). He didn't know where he was going. He didn't know how long it would take for him to get there. He didn't even know how God would carry out His promise.

> Can you think of a time God called you to follow Him when you didn't know all of the details? Describe how you felt and what you did.

While Abram didn't know all the details, God's call to follow Him included promises that He would honor:

ABRAM'S RESPONSIBILITY	GOD'S PROMISES
"Go from your country and your kindred and your father's house ..." (Genesis 12:1)	*"... I will show you [the land]"* (Genesis 12:1) *"I will make of you a great nation ..."* (Genesis 12:2) *"... I will bless you and make your name great"* (Genesis 12:2) *"I will bless those who bless you, and him who dishonors you I will curse, and in you all the families of the earth shall be blessed."* (Genesis 12:3)

Following God requires faith. Scripture reveals that in his lifetime, Abram did not receive all the things God promised but *"greeted them from afar"* (Hebrews 11:13). In faith, he followed God from the known to the unknown (Hebrews 11:8).

As Abram passed through the land God promised to him, in Genesis 12:6-7 he came to a place that would be marked in the future as a place of decision.[1] In the years to come, Shechem would be where Abram's descendents, the Israelites, assembled to choose between God's promises of blessings or curses (Deuteronomy 11:29-30). It is also at Shechem where the kingdom of Israel later broke into two (1 Kings 12), pointing to the need for a better kingdom, one referred to in the New Testament as *"a kingdom that cannot be shaken"* (Hebrews 12:28). This is the Kingdom of Christ: a son of Abraham (Matthew 1:1) who has truly blessed *"all the families of the earth"* (Genesis 12:3).

To follow God's guidance required a decision of faith and obedience from Abram, and the same is true for us today. With the internet at our fingertips and information moving at its fastest pace in history, we often desire all of the details before we're willing to follow God's lead. But the Bible tells us without faith it is impossible to please God (Hebrews 11:6).

Not only do we seek God's guidance, but we have to choose to follow Him wherever He leads. Like Abram, we may not always know where God is taking us. Still, we can cling to God's promise to guide us, walk in daily obedience, and by faith follow Jesus one step at a time.

DAY 7

EXODUS 14: God will remind you that He made a way when it seemed like there was no way.

Today's reading does not include a direct promise to the modern reader, though it contains several of God's specific promises to the Israelites: *"I will get glory over Pharaoh"* (Exodus 14:4), *"see the salvation of the LORD, which he will work for you today"* (Exodus 14:13), and *"the LORD will fight for you"* (Exodus 14:14). These were all guaranteed promises that came true for Israel.

The principle they illustrate for us today is just as true: God made a way to salvation when it seemed like there was no way. Today's reading teaches us something very important about God's promise to guide His children.

Before we get into Exodus 14, let's do a quick recap of what happened to God's people up to this point:

Israel had spent 400 years enslaved in Egypt (Exodus 1:11). God sent Moses to free His people and lead them to the land He had promised their ancestor Abraham (Exodus 3:1-17). By the end of Exodus 13, Pharaoh released God's people from slavery in Egypt, and God led Israel into the wilderness toward the Red Sea (Exodus 13:17-18).

The final verses of Exodus 13 detail how God led the people: *"And the LORD went before them by day in a pillar of cloud to lead them along the way, and by night in a pillar of fire to give them light, that they might travel by day and by night"* (v. 21). Because of God's guidance, Israel could travel at any time and be confident they were heading in the right direction.

With this in mind, let's join Israel in Exodus 14. According to verse 2, God led them to encamp between Migdol and the Red Sea.

> Based on verses 3-4, what did God know would happen because of His decision to lead Israel to this place?

God intentionally led His people to a place that would put them squarely in between an army much stronger than they were and a sea impossible for them to cross on their own. Even though they had just witnessed deliverance from Egypt by God's hand, the people panicked and doubted God's guidance (Exodus 14:10-12).

In spite of the people's fear, God's plan remained the same.

According to verse 15, how did God answer their cry?

God made a way where it seemed like there was no way. The Bible is full of examples of God guiding His children through things that, in human terms, appeared impossible:

- God parted the Red Sea and made a path of dry land for Israel to cross (Exodus 14:21-23).
- God brought Shadrach, Meshach and Abednego through a fiery furnace (Daniel 3:8-26).
- God guided the prophet Daniel through a lion's den (Daniel 6).
- Jesus made a way for His disciple Peter to walk on the water (Matthew 14:22-33).
- God broke chains and opened prison cells for the Apostle Paul (Acts 16:23-33).
- God rolled back the stone of Jesus' tomb, resurrected His Son, and made a way for us to live eternally with Him (Matthew 28:1-8).

In today's reading, not only did God's plan for Israel bring Him glory over Pharaoh (Exodus 14:4), but God also used His guidance through the Red Sea to teach His people.

According to Exodus 14:31, what did Israel see, and how did they respond?

How does knowing this truth — that God can make a way when we don't see a way — help you go forward and follow Him today?

Today's scriptures show us that we can pray for anything and everything. Nothing is too hard for God! At the same time, He may not always answer every prayer in the way we desire when we ask Him to change our circumstances or remove barriers here on earth. Some paths may always be blocked in this life. But even then, we can trust it is for our good (Romans 8:28). Most importantly, there is one way that looked forever lost to us but is now gloriously torn open for us. This way remains open while we are alive and until Christ returns: the way to God through faith in Christ.

Those who trust in Jesus have access to His guidance now and forever. That's a promise we can count on!

DAY 8

JOHN 8:12-30: God will light the way so you do not stumble.

In John 8:12b, Jesus gives two promises to His people:

1. We *"will not walk in darkness."*
2. We *"will have the light of life."*

Participation alert! ● In order for us to experience these promises, Jesus noted something we must do.

> For context, the beginning of verse 12 says, *"Again Jesus spoke to them,"* referring to a group of Jewish religious law experts. But notice that Jesus' promise isn't conditional on expertise … What condition did Jesus actually give for these promises?

Yesterday we read about God's guidance of Israel out of Egypt. Today, as we open the pages of John 8, we see Jesus said something to a Jewish crowd that would have immediately brought to mind their exodus out of Egypt.

Jesus announced, *"I am the light of the world"* (John 8:12a) — and this took place during the Feast of Tabernacles in Israel. During this feast, lamps were lit at the tabernacle to remind God's people of how He led them through the wilderness by night in a pillar of fire.[1]

In the exodus, God physically led His people from slavery to freedom in the promised land. Jesus' claim to be the Light of the world represents spiritual guidance and freedom found in Him alone.

> In verse 13, the Pharisees tried to discredit Jesus' promise by saying, *"You are bearing witness about yourself."* In response, what did Jesus say about who He is and who sent Him (vv. 18, 23, 28)? How does this reassure us that His promises are still true today?

Here are three ways the light of Christ guides our lives:

1. The guiding light of His Word. We can count on His Word to be a lamp for our feet (Psalm 119:105). The Word of God provides a spiritual light to guide us in the way we should go.

> When you seek guidance for a decision in your life or a choice between behaviors, do you usually look for an answer in God's Word? Why or why not?

2. The illuminating light of His Truth. In the chapter following Jesus' claim to be the Light of the world, John records how Jesus healed a blind man (John 9). Sadly, many of God's very people in Israel were blind to the Truth of Jesus as the Light of the world and salvation for their souls (John 8:13; John 8:19). But we can ask God to give us eyes to see and know the Truth today (Matthew 13:16).

> We could start by crying out the words of Psalm 139:23a: *"Search me, O God, and know my heart!"* When was the last time you asked God to open the eyes of your heart to the blind spots in your life?

3. The safety of His light. Walking in darkness is a natural metaphor for stumbling – but because Jesus is the Light of the world, we can confidently follow Him and trust He will make our paths straight (Proverbs 3:6). As we follow Him, Jesus will guide us into the Truth of His Word (John 12:35-36) and help us not to stumble into sin.

> Which one of these three ways will you seek God today as you cling to the biblical promise of Jesus as the Light of your life?

DAY 9

JOHN 16:5-15: God will guide you when the road ahead feels uncertain.

Today's promise from God is painted on a backdrop of grief, anxiousness and confusion. Jesus' disciples had just heard disturbing details about the future that awaited them: They would face persecution and hatred from the world (John 15:18-19; John 16:2), and Jesus revealed He would soon be returning to His Father (John 16:5).

The disciples didn't want Jesus to leave them, yet Jesus assured them it was for their good because His death, resurrection and ascension to the Father would usher the presence of the Holy Spirit into the heart of every believer in Jesus.

> In the midst of an unknown, uncertain future, what promise did Jesus give His disciples in John 16:7?

> According to John 16:13, what would the Helper (*"Spirit of truth"*) do?

Jesus promised to send the Helper, or Holy Spirit, to be in close fellowship with His disciples — a spiritual fellowship even better than the physical access they'd had to Jesus on earth. The Spirit speaks to God's people only what He hears from Jesus and the Father; therefore, He is our direct line of communication with the Lord. The Holy Spirit is also our Guide so we will not be caught off guard by things present or future (John 16:1; John 16:13).

The same Helper promised to Jesus' first disciples is promised to us today. The Holy Spirit guides us into all Truth and gives us deep, direct connection to the heart and mind of Jesus.

> Read the following scriptures about the Holy Spirit, and note what He does. How does this fulfill the promise Jesus made in John 16?
>
> **EPHESIANS 1:13:**

ACTS 1:8:

ROMANS 8:16:

A few things are important to consider about following the guidance of the Holy Spirit in our lives:

1. To follow our Guide, we must acknowledge we don't know the way. Maybe you're the type of person who doesn't like to ask for directions, preferring to seek help from your GPS app when you're going someplace new or even somewhere you've been before …

But in order to receive the guidance promised us by the Holy Spirit, we must be willing to admit we don't hold the future. Sometimes we feel like we're traversing through the wilderness where there is no clear path or direction; this was an accurate depiction of the future for Jesus' first disciples, and the same is true for us today. It is in these kinds of circumstances when the significance of our Guide becomes very clear.

2. The goal of the Spirit's guidance is not to take us where we want to go but to glorify Jesus. The Holy Spirit reveals God's Word and His ways to us. His goal is not to give us what we want but to inform us of what God says and thereby glorify Jesus (John 16:14).

> When have you experienced tension between something you really wanted for your life and something God wanted? How has the Holy Spirit helped guide you through this tension — or how could you ask Him to guide you today?

When the road ahead feels uncertain, sometimes we're inclined to tighten our grip on the steering wheel of our life. But the guidance of the Holy Spirit often takes us in directions we didn't imagine or expect. When we remember these two things about following His guidance, it helps us loosen our grip of control and cling to God's promise of guidance.

DAY 10

JAMES 1: God will give you wisdom when you need it.

Dr. Tony Evans describes wisdom as the ability to apply biblical Truth to life decisions so you don't live life independent of God.[1] In other words, it's the right truth used the right way at the right time.

Each day we are faced with decisions and choices that require God's wisdom, and according to today's reading, that wisdom is readily available to us. James 1:5 breaks down how and to whom God gives wisdom.

> In the verse below, underline **who** God gives wisdom to. Circle **how** He gives wisdom.

> *"If any of you lacks wisdom, let him ask God, who gives generously to all without reproach, and it will be given him"* (James 1:5).

The original Greek word for *"generously"* is used only here in all of Scripture. It implies that God's giving is "led solely by his desire to bless."[2] The Greek word ἁπλῶς (*haplōs*) could also be translated "without reserve, liberally, abundantly, bountifully or lavishly."

Not only does God give generously, but James notes that He also gives graciously to all. Scholar Douglas Moo explains it like this: "He does not reprimand us for past failures or remind us endlessly of the value of the gifts he gives."[3]

> Describe a time when you may have felt disqualified from receiving God's wisdom. How does James 1:5 change your perspective?

The wisdom of God is available to us at any time on any occasion; however, once again, we find a promise that requires our participation.

> According to James 1:5-6, what two things must we do to receive the promised wisdom from God?

To receive the promise of wisdom from God, we must *ask*. It's interesting to note that much of the book of James addresses trials and the testing of our faith (James 1:2-4; James 1:12-15) – and sometimes when we face tests, we might be inclined to lean on our own resources or understanding. Or we might busy our minds with worry and forget the promise of God's wisdom. But many scholars believe James wrote with Jesus' words from Matthew 7:7 in mind: *"Ask, and it will be given to you; seek, and you will find; knock, and it will be opened to you."*

What are you worrying about or trying to solve right now?

Use the space below to write a prayer surrendering your own efforts in these areas and asking God to give you His wisdom for the situations you described above.

After we ask, we also must not doubt (James 1:6). The meaning of the original Greek word for "doubt" in James 1 points to a "division within the believer that brings about wavering and inconsistency of attitude toward God."[1] James' call to ask and not doubt is one that requires active faith.

No, we are not promised immediate results when we ask. We are not promised that God's wisdom will be given exactly as we expect it. However, when we ask, we can trust that God *will* do what He said He will do.

Later in James 1, we're reminded why we can ask and not doubt. James said, *"Every good gift and every perfect gift is from above, coming down from the Father of lights, with whom there is no variation or shadow due to change"* (James 1:17). Because God is perfect and never changes, we can trust that He will give us wisdom when we ask.

WEEKEND REFLECTION
WEEK 2

As we close our study on God's promises of guidance this week, let's think about a simple illustration to help us remember how following God's guidance requires our submission to Him.

How do you feel when someone else is driving your car? Relaxed and at ease? Or a bit anxious and on edge? When we hand over the keys and let someone else drive, we may feel like since we're not in control of the car, we need to offer suggestions about which way to go, or at times, we may correct what we believe the driver could do better.

But what about when you drive young children somewhere? When children are in the back seat and their parents or trusted adults are driving, they often don't even look ahead to see where the car is going. They talk with each other and laugh. They sing along with the music on the radio, color, or read a book.

Their ride down the road is much more enjoyable.

This metaphor isn't perfect since God does give us decisions to make in our lives, so we're not just passively along for the ride — but at the same time, to follow God's guidance in many ways requires us to sit in the passenger seat as we let Him lead. As we travel ahead, let's do less resisting of God's guidance and more resting in Him.

PRAYING THE PROMISES (PSALM 25:4-5, 9-10)
Dear God, thank You that You lead the humble in what is right and teach the humble Your way. Help me humble myself before You. Show me Your paths, that I may walk in the way of Your steadfast love and faithfulness. "Lead me in your truth and teach me, for you are the God of my salvation" (v. 5). I will wait expectantly for Your guidance. In Jesus' name, amen.

NOTES

NOTES

WEEK THREE

PROMISE OF COMFORT

DAY 11

GENESIS 16: God will always see you.

Today's reading is another Old Testament story that circles back to Abram's family (remember how we talked about God's promise to him on Day 6?). But today's reading includes some new characters.

List any details you find about these people and the roles they play in the story:

CHARACTER	DETAILS
1) Sarai	
2) Hagar	
3) Ishmael	

In the space below, record what Sarai said in Genesis 16:2 (keeping in mind what God promised back in Genesis 12:1-3).

Just one chapter before this, God had answered Abram's questions about the promises God had given to him (Genesis 15:1-11). In addition, God Himself established a covenant with Abram and affirmed the promises (Genesis 15:12-21). Yet as Genesis 16 opens, we find Sarai and Abram trying to realize God's promises by way of their own plans.

Instead of following God's voice, whose voice did Abram listen to (Genesis 16:2)?

Describe a time you listened to the voice of someone else instead of following God's voice. What was the result?

Sarai's plan didn't unfold as she hoped. Instead, it created tension and greater heartache that eventually led Hagar to run away from Sarai's harsh treatment (Genesis 16:4-6). Human effort alone will never fulfill divine promise.

Pregnant, rejected and alone in the wilderness, Hagar encountered *"the angel of the Lord"* by a spring of water (Genesis 16:7). According to many scholars, this encounter was a theophany — a moment when God appeared to a human being.[1] Other examples of theophany include when God appeared to Moses in the burning bush (Exodus 3:2-4) and when He appeared to Gideon (Judges 6:11-18).

In Genesis 16:10-12, what did God promise Hagar?

Based on what we've already learned about contextualizing Bible promises, we can identify these promises as specific to Hagar and therefore not intended to apply directly to us today. However, we can see the principle of **why** God promised to comfort Hagar and multiply her family — because He *"listened to [her] affliction"* (v. 11) — and we know He listens to us when we are suffering today.

Read the following scriptural examples of God **seeing** and **hearing** His people, and note how His seeing and hearing relates to His promise keeping:

EXODUS 2:23-25:

PSALM 106:43-45:

When Hagar felt unseen and forgotten, the God of the universe pursued her and comforted her in her time of need. Hagar called Him *El-Roi*, or "the God who sees me."[2] This is the only time in all of Scripture where a human being ascribes a name to God.[3]

It's also interesting to note how God comforted Hagar: He did not change her circumstances (Genesis 16:9). Instead, He called Hagar's attention away from her past hurts and toward His future promises (Genesis 16:10-12).

Like Hagar, in our times of affliction, we can take comfort in *El-Roi* — the God who sees us.

DAY 12

EZEKIEL 34:11-24: God will diligently care for you.

In Ezekiel 34:7-11, in the middle of a prophecy against corrupt leaders in ancient Israel (whom God characterized as selfish shepherds), God claimed ownership of His sheep, or His people, and made several specific statements about what He would do for His flock.

In verse 16 alone, God made six "I will" promises. Fill in the blanks below with what God said He would do:

I will _____.

I will _____.

I will _____.

I will _____.

I will _____.

I will _____.

Read the verses surrounding verse 16, and record more of God's "I will" statements below. How does knowing God's heart for His people bring you comfort?

God would not entrust His people to selfish shepherds (Ezekiel 34:7-10). He would search for and seek out His sheep (v. 11). The Hebrew word translated *"seek ... out"* in verse 11 is בָּקַר *(baqar)*, a root word Ezekiel also uses twice in verse 12 to convey the idea of careful examination of the sheep's condition, motivated by God's desire to seek the welfare of His flock.[1]

Ezekiel 34 contrasts our heavenly Shepherd against human shepherds (leaders) who exploit, neglect and mistreat their sheep. Have you ever trusted someone you thought was a good shepherd, only to find out they weren't? Consider taking a moment to bring those wounds before the Lord. Write your prayer below, and receive God's promise that He is a Shepherd who will *never* let you down.

The role of a shepherd in the Ancient Near East included feeding, guiding, shielding and supporting one's sheep. Sheep depended on their shepherd for essentially everything and were considered helpless in the absence of a shepherd.

> With this in mind, the imagery in today's reading recalls David's words in Psalm 23 ("The Lord Is My Shepherd"). Read Psalm 23, and note how it echoes God's promises in Ezekiel 34.

> After declaring that God was his Shepherd in Psalm 23:1-3, how did David feel in verse 4? How might declaring and believing God's promises affect our emotions similarly?

The rod and the staff that comforted David (Psalm 23:4) would have been familiar tools for him, as he was a shepherd before he became king of Israel (1 Samuel 17:34-35). Shepherds used a staff both to keep count of their sheep and to navigate the terrain on which they traveled (Leviticus 27:32). And the shepherd's rod defended the flock against predators (Ezekiel 20:37).

As we close today's study, let's touch on one more responsibility of a shepherd: Along with the *comfort* of the shepherd's rod and staff, there was also *confidence* that the shepherd would find sheep that were lost (Ezekiel 34:11-12; Luke 19:10).

If you feel lost today, remember God's promise, and take comfort: God sees you and is seeking you. Our Shepherd will not always remove us from shadows and valleys, but He promises to guide and protect us through the darkness (Psalm 23:4).

DAY 13

JOHN 10:1-18: God will comfort you with His voice.

One way to define "comfort" is as a state of satisfaction or physical well-being provided by a person or thing, which also includes a feeling of freedom from worry or disappointment. With this in mind, we'll find that today's reading details the kind of comfort God's sheep receive from the sound of their Shepherd's voice.

> After reading today's Bible passage about Jesus, what connections do you see to God's promises in Ezekiel 34 that we studied yesterday? Why do you think these connections between Old Testament and New Testament promises are important?

The opening verses of John 10 record Jesus' words to some religious law experts who were questioning who He was. In response, Jesus used a *"figure of speech"* (John 10:6) to reveal His identity. First, he described a sheep pen where several different flocks of sheep had gathered. This scene was not uncommon during Jesus' time. On these occasions, a shepherd would enter through the gate and call out his sheep by their individual names.

D.A. Carson explains: "Unlike Western shepherds who drive the sheep, often using a sheep dog, the shepherds of the Near East, both now and in Jesus' day, lead their flocks, their voice calling them on … The sheep follow simply because they know his voice."[1]

In stark contrast, the sheep would run from a voice they did not recognize (John 10:5). But there was a familiarity and comfort with the sound of a shepherd's voice that would lead his sheep to follow him (John 10:3).

This kind of knowing was more than simply recognition: The comfort of the shepherd's voice derived from the knowing of *experience*.

> Think of some voices in your life that you know well and can easily identify. Why do you know these voices so well?

Does God's voice feel familiar and easily identifiable to you? Why or why not?

The sheep knew their shepherd's voice because they spent time with him. They received tender care from his hand and enjoyed the green pastures of his provision. They walked safe paths to still waters and rested in the protection of his rod of comfort.

In John 10:11 and verse 14, Jesus revealed Himself as the Good Shepherd; He promised to *"lay down [His] life for the sheep"* (John 10:15) and to save all who come to the Father through Him (John 10:9). To experience the promised comfort of our Good Shepherd's voice, we need more than just an informational knowledge of Jesus. We need to know Him in our minds *and* experience Him in our hearts to enjoy a relationship with Him.

When the world feels loud and we're desperate for the comfort of our Shepherd's voice, here are a few steps we can take to help us hear Him call us by name:

1. **Look for ways to silence other voices.** From social media feeds to the latest show we're streaming, our lives are oftentimes bombarded with noise. It will be easier to find comfort from our Shepherd's voice when we quiet other voices to hear His more clearly.
2. **Prioritize spending time with our Shepherd.** The more time we spend with Jesus by praying and reading His Word, the more familiar His voice will become.

    What is one way you will practically silence other sounds in your life today to listen for Jesus' voice?

    How can you prioritize spending time with Jesus more than you already do? Could you read your Bible right before you fall asleep instead of scrolling through social media? Could you pray right when you open your eyes in the morning instead of checking the weather forecast?

DAY 14

1 PETER 5:1-11: God will carry all of your burdens and worries.

Today's reading begins with the now-familiar imagery of shepherds leading their flocks. In this passage, the Apostle Peter specifically exhorted the elders or leaders of the early Church to shepherd God's people willingly and faithfully (1 Peter 5:1-3).

After addressing the elders directly, Peter then turned his attention to the entire congregation. He urged them to be humble (1 Peter 5:5-6), then reminded them of the care God promises to us when we give Him our worries and concerns (1 Peter 5:7).

The believers to whom Peter wrote were facing trials and suffering (1 Peter 5:8-9). Peter consoled them with three promises:

1. God cares for His people (1 Peter 5:7).
2. Even in suffering, God's people are not alone (1 Peter 5:9).
3. God will restore, confirm, strengthen and establish His people (1 Peter 5:10).

Enjoying the blessings of these three promises requires our participation! •

The second and third promises require us to be sober-minded and watchful to actively resist the devil. Returning to the sheep/shepherd metaphor, Peter described our adversary like a roaring lion looking for unguarded sheep to devour (1 Peter 5:8-9). In order to resist his attack, we are called to live sober-minded — cautious against sin and alert to the schemes of the devil at all times.

> What else do the scriptures below say about lions threatening God's people? How does this give you confidence in God's promise to care for you as you follow Him?
>
> **1 SAMUEL 17:37:**
>
>
> **DANIEL 6:22:**
>
>
> **ISAIAH 35:8-9:**

Let's spend the rest of our time today unwrapping the first promise in today's reading: God cares for us. The comfort we receive from God's care results from casting our cares on Him (1 Peter 5:7).

Jesus also talked to His disciples about casting their cares on Him:

"I tell you, do not be anxious about your life, what you will eat or what you will drink, nor about your body, what you will put on. Is not life more than food, and the body more than clothing? Look at the birds of the air: they neither sow nor reap nor gather into barns, and yet your heavenly Father feeds them. Are you not of more value than they? And which of you by being anxious can add a single hour to his span of life?" (Matthew 6:25-27).

What did Jesus tell His listeners *not* to do?

Jesus asked three questions in these verses. Record those in your own words below.

How would your life be different today if you cast your burdens and worries on Jesus and let Him care for you?

The practical actions connected to these promises are wrapped up in one major heart position — humility (1 Peter 5:5-6). We receive the comfort of God when we are willing to humble ourselves before Him, recognizing our limits and relying on our limitless God. Humility highlights our need for Jesus and prompts us to cast our cares on Him (1 Peter 5:7).

DAY 15

2 CORINTHIANS 1:1-11: God will comfort you in your troubles.

In today's reading in the New Testament, the Apostle Paul used the word *"comfort"* 10 times in verses 3-7 alone. Six times in these same verses, he also used the words *"affliction"* or *"suffer[ing]."*

Beginning in verse 8, Paul revealed some details about his own sufferings in the province of Asia — where he traveled as a missionary for Christ but apparently met violent opposition — as well as how God comforted him and his companions in those trials.

> According to 2 Corinthians 1:8-9, how did Paul and his companions feel?

With words like *"burdened beyond our strength,"* Paul described circumstances that crushed and overwhelmed them and seemed impossible to endure. Their troubles were so excruciating that Paul and his fellow believers feared they would not live through them (2 Corinthians 1:8).

It is out of trials like this that Paul wrote to the church in Corinth about comfort.

> After reading about Paul's torment, we might hope for a promise like, "Don't worry — God will protect you from this kind of suffering." But instead, what two things does Paul promise *"you will also share"* (v. 7)?

> What seems reassuring about this promise, and what feels undesirable or troubling?

Following God doesn't exempt us from all suffering – and in fact, like Paul's life demonstrates, sometimes following God leads us *into* suffering for His sake. But God does promise us His comfort no matter what happens. And we can learn three truths about this comfort from today's passage:

1. God is the source of every comfort, consolation and encouragement (2 Corinthians 1:3). If God is the *only* source for *every* comfort, we must acknowledge that any source of comfort we seek apart from Him is either temporary or altogether false. No amount of earthly balm will ultimately ease the pain of our hardships. Only the comfort of God will truly come through for us in our times of desperation.

2. As sufferings increase, God's comfort increases (2 Corinthians 1:5). Paul drew attention to two significant components of comfort and suffering: First, when we suffer, we share in the sufferings of Jesus. Our hardship is not unknown to our Savior. Second, in the abundance of trouble, we can also expect abundance of God's comfort. The New Living Translation says it this way: *"The more we suffer for Christ, the more God will shower us with his comfort through Christ"* (v. 5).

3. God comforts us so we can comfort others (2 Corinthians 1:4). Paul recorded some blessings that came out of his experience of God's comfort in suffering: He and his companions learned to trust God and stop relying on themselves (2 Corinthians 1:9). Because of God's comfort, Paul was also able to comfort the members of the church in Corinth (v. 4).

We cannot find true comfort apart from God, but we can be the conduit of God's comfort for each other. As the comfort of God moved through Paul to the church in Corinth, so also the Corinthians helped Paul through their prayers (v. 11). The God of all comfort allows His people to show His comfort to one another.

> Think of a time God has comforted you. How can you use your experience to be a vessel of God's promised comfort for someone today?

WEEKEND REFLECTION
WEEK 3

This week, we've studied God's promises that we are seen, carried, comforted and cared for by God Himself. To look to anything else for comfort is futile and will never truly ease our pain. This may remind you of what we learned in the introduction of our study about the differences between God's promises, which always come true and always satisfy our souls, and the promises of sin, which never do.

Sometimes, when we are hurting, the devil crouches nearby in search of wounded prey. He tells us that we can find the comfort we need in an activity or in a bad habit or in the arms of another person. All the while, God's arms are ready and waiting to scoop us up and care for us.

If you're hurting today, remember you're not alone. The Israelites needed comfort. Peter and Paul needed comfort. The church in Corinth needed comfort. At some point, we all need comfort. So let's turn to Jesus, our Good Shepherd, and listen for His voice. Let Him hold you, comfort you, and lead you through the valley today.

PRAYING THE PROMISES (PSALM 23)
Oh Lord, You are my Shepherd who comforts me. You feed me, guide me and shield me. In You, I have all that I need. Bring me to rest in green pastures. Lead me beside quiet waters. Refresh and restore my soul. Even when I walk through the valley of the shadow of death, I will not fear. Bring me comfort today with Your protection and guidance. In Jesus' name, amen.

NOTES

NOTES

CLINGING TO GOD'S PROMISES WHEN YOU FACE SUFFERING

Dear God, today I am facing pain and hardship in these areas of my life:

To cling to Your promises, I will remember Your Word says:

"For I consider that the sufferings of this present time are not worth comparing with the glory that is to be revealed to us" *(Romans 8:18).*

"And after you have suffered a little while, the God of all grace, who has called you to his eternal glory in Christ, will himself restore, confirm, strengthen, and establish you" *(1 Peter 5:10).*

"For this light momentary affliction is preparing for us an eternal weight of glory beyond all comparison …" *(2 Corinthians 4:17).*

"Beloved, do not be surprised at the fiery trial when it comes upon you to test you, as though something strange were happening to you. But rejoice insofar as you share Christ's sufferings, that you may also rejoice and be glad when his glory is revealed" *(1 Peter 4:12-13).*

"For as we share abundantly in Christ's sufferings, so through Christ we share abundantly in comfort too" *(2 Corinthians 1:5).*

In Jesus' name, amen.

WEEK FOUR

PROMISE OF STRENGTH

DAY 16

GENESIS 17:1-21: God will never fail you.

The Hebrew name for God Almighty is *El Shaddai*. The exact original meaning of *El Shaddai* is difficult to determine; however, proposed meanings include "The Powerful, Strong One" and "The One Who Suffices."[1] In today's Scripture study, we're checking back in with Abram in Genesis 17, where God — *El Shaddai* — showed His power, might and sufficiency in several ways.

First, God displayed His strength to change **circumstances**.

> How old was Abram when God reiterated His promise of a son (Genesis 17:1-2)? How old was Abram's wife, Sarai (Genesis 17:17)?

As God reaffirmed His promise to give Abram a son and bless him with offspring too many to count, Abram saw the reality of his current circumstances. Far beyond childbearing years, Abram questioned whether his physical limitations were insurmountable (Genesis 17:17). But God Almighty could make Abram the father of nations — and only by His power was it accomplished (Genesis 21:1-7).

God also displayed His power to change **identity**.

Between the first and the last verses of Genesis 17, the identities of both Abram and Sarai were changed forever.

> In verse 5, God changed Abram's name, and in verse 15, God changed Sarai's name. What new names did God give them?

63

Names carried great significance in Old Testament times. The name "Abraham" in Hebrew meant "father of a multitude" and therefore pointed to God's promise of many offspring.[2] Sarai is actually the only woman in the Bible to receive a new name, and her new name, Sarah, was connected to the Hebrew word for "princess" and the promise in Genesis 17:16 that she would bear kings.[3]

> Of course, the new identities God gave Abraham and Sarah were specifically for them. But in 2 Corinthians 5:17 we find a timeless promise of new identity. Who is this promise for?

Today's reading also includes God's covenant of circumcision (Genesis 17:10-14) — which we may be tempted to read with a nervous "yikes!" and a quick turn of the page in our Bibles. But let's think about how this promise, too, shows us God's unfailing character:

> Read Deuteronomy 30:6 and Ezekiel 36:26. When you consider how believers in Jesus are transformed by Him today, how do these verses show that God has kept His promise?

God alone is sufficient to keep His promises. To be sufficient is to be *enough*. By His own sufficiency, God kept His promise to make Abraham a great nation. In light of this specific promise to Abraham, we find a principle we can hold on to right now:

God's strength never fails. He did not fail Abraham and Sarah, and He will not fail us today.

The God Almighty who kept His promise to Abraham and Sarah, the God Almighty who changed their circumstances and their identity, is the same God Almighty today. He is most powerful and able to do anything at any time for His glory and our good.

DAY 17

ISAIAH 41:1-20: God will hold you up when you are afraid.

Today's reading creates a sharp contrast between those who trust in false gods created by humans (Isaiah 41:1-7) and those who hope in the Lord (Isaiah 41:8-20).

For those who find their strength in false gods, theologian John Oswalt describes the devastating reality like this: "In the face of the terror coming from the east, it is not the gods who strengthen their worshipers but the worshipers must strengthen each other and eventually the idols themselves."[1]

But for the children of God, the promise of Isaiah 41:10 defines a much different reality.

> According to Isaiah 41:8-10, what were God's chosen people not to do, and why?

> What promises from God can we lean on so that we will not fear or dismay? (As a reminder, scriptures like 1 Peter 2:9 affirm that all who trust in Jesus today are spiritual descendants of Israel and are also chosen by God!)

Because God was their God and He was with them, the people of Israel at the time of Isaiah's prophecy didn't have to look around and be afraid. Instead, they could count on the three "I will" statements from God in verse 10:

1. *"I will strengthen you."*
2. *"I will help you."*
3. *"I will uphold you."*

> What other "I will" promises does God make in verses 17-20? How do these promises further reveal God as a provider, protector and redeemer who holds up His people?

Each of these statements includes a promised action from God for His people. Their hope was not in happy thoughts about the future. Instead, they could find their strength in the expectation that God Himself would act on their behalf.

When we couple Isaiah 41:10 with what the prophet wrote in verse 13, a still more beautiful picture develops.

> What does verse 10 say God does with His right hand? In verse 13, what does God do with His left hand?

Of this image, Oswalt says: "Taken together, these two verses present a powerful picture of parent and child: in the father's right hand is a mighty weapon to defeat any enemy, but his left hand is holding the child's right [hand]."[2]

Think of the children you know and how they hold their parents' hands — when walking, sitting by each other, at a ball game or in the living room. Many times in busy or unknown places, parents encourage their children to hold on tight, leading them safely through a crowd or across a street.

When children are scared, they also often reach for a parent's hand. Whether during a thunderstorm or on a roller coaster, something about holding mom or dad's hand makes our little ones feel safer and stronger.

That's what God's hand is for us. When we feel weak, when the road ahead is unknown, or when we're afraid, we can cling to God's promise: *I will hold you up*.

DAY 18

JOHN 6:22-58: God will sustain you.

In today's reading, Jesus was speaking to crowds that had been following Him and listening to His teachings, and not long after miraculously feeding 5,000 people with five loaves and two fish, He announced Himself as the Bread of Life (John 6:35). His proclamation included several promises.

Verse 35 says that whoever comes to Jesus in faith:

1. "Shall not hunger."
2. "Shall never thirst."

Jesus identified Himself as the sustaining strength we need to live. His proclamation recalled God's past provision of manna for His people as they traveled in the wilderness (John 6:31; Exodus 16:4) yet also stood in contrast to the crowd's present desire for physical sustenance and satisfaction.

> According to John 6:22-26, why did the crowd come to Jesus?

> In verse 27, what did Jesus tell them *not* to work for? What did He say to work for instead?

As the Bread of Life, Jesus strengthens and supports more than just our bodies. Jesus is the sustenance for our souls. Because Jesus is the Bread of Life, we don't have to depend on physical sustenance alone to supply our strength. We can feast in times of plenty, but we can also feast in the wilderness.

> In what ways do you rely on God to sustain you with physical resources in your life?
> In what ways do you rely on Him to sustain you spiritually?

Interestingly, we see lots of images of bread and food throughout Scripture. In Psalm 63:5, David wrote, *"My soul will be satisfied as with fat and rich food, and my mouth will praise you with joyful lips."* This verse invites us to imagine a feast: a lavish table beautifully decorated and full of the finest foods.

But when we read the verses that surround this one, it creates a very different setting. Instead of a feast, we see a famine: *"My soul thirsts for you; my flesh faints for you, as in a dry and weary land where there is no water"* (Psalm 63:1).

None of us would ever wish for the wilderness. But Scripture shows us that, thankfully, feasting on the Bread of Life is not reserved for the choicest of circumstances.

In fact, after Jesus Himself once fasted for 40 days and nights in the wilderness, He was physically famished and still gave us an example of the sustenance found in God alone. Satan came and tempted Jesus to transform stones into bread to eat (Matthew 4:3), but Jesus resisted the devil's temptation with this response: *"It is written, 'Man shall not live by bread alone, but by every word that comes from the mouth of God'"* (Matthew 4:4).

> Here's a great example of why we take care to faithfully interpret promises in Scripture! Based on Matthew 4:4 and John 6:27, if we don't read carefully, it might sound like God's people don't need to eat food to survive. How would you combat this misinterpretation if someone presented it to you? How would you explain the true meaning of these promises?

Here's a simple story to illustrate the point of this study day: Imagine you meet two women who follow Jesus in completely different circumstances and on opposite sides of the country. Both of these women may speak about difficult circumstances, unanswered questions and uncertainties they face, yet both could also speak of the satisfaction they find in God's Word.

They may not speak of one moment that seemed to change everything for them, but instead each could gush about God's faithfulness and the strength that comes only from meeting with Him day after day, week after week, month after month, year after year, in His Word.

In the end, we don't find our sustenance from the fullness of our circumstances; instead, we feast on the rich portion of God's Word. When our circumstances leave us empty, we can find strength in Jesus, the Bread of Life.

DAY 19

2 CORINTHIANS 12:1-10: God will be your strength when you are weak.

Two key words permeate today's reading yet don't seem to go together well: *"boasting"* and *"weakness."*

In 2 Corinthians 12, the Apostle Paul was writing to a church in Corinth that was struggling with issues of pride, division, and confusion caused by false prophets, and he taught them how to be content — not in strength but in weakness. He even took it one step further and claimed to *"boast"* in weakness (2 Corinthians 12:9).

It seems difficult to wrap our minds around such a concept. Our culture rarely, if ever, demonstrates this. Social media feeds don't boast of all we *can't* do. They highlight what we've done. Recognition is not awarded to the weak, but it's reserved for the strongest, most capable person. Weakness is simply something we do not accept, much less boast about.

> According to 2 Corinthians 12:10, why did Paul determine that it is good to boast in weakness?

Paul spoke of a specific weakness, *"a thorn ... in the flesh,"* that harassed him so severely he pleaded with God to remove it three times (2 Corinthians 12:7-8).

> Is there something in your life you have pleaded with the Lord to change or take away? Describe those circumstances below.

God chose not to remove this point of pain for Paul.

> What reason did Paul give for God's choice not to remove the thorn in his flesh (v. 7)? In verse 9, what promise did God make about His power?

Because Paul was so aware of his weakness, he did not, and could not, rely on himself for strength. His weaknesses required him to rely wholly on God's power and strength.

If we want to truly experience the promise of God's strength, we, too, are called to stop relying on ourselves and rely fully on God. To help us shift our reliance from ourselves to our Savior, let's look at a few of symptoms of self-reliance:

— Our thoughts swarm around our to-do lists all day.
— We say things like "I'm fine" when we know we're really not, or "I've got this" when, deep down, we really don't.
— We'd rather walk across hot coals than ask someone for help.
— When life gets hectic, the time we spend with our Father is the first thing we drop.

Ouch! We're stepping on our own toes as we write this. We didn't have to think very hard to list these signs of attempted self-sufficiency ... because unfortunately, we all find them sneaking into our lives.

> Are you experiencing any of these symptoms today? Which ones are most common in your life?

Self-reliance can show itself in all the things we take on our own shoulders and rely on ourselves to solve, fix or arrange ... and also in all the things we refuse to take on because we can't figure out how to solve, fix or arrange them. In either situation, we are allowing an inaccurate definition of "strength" to control our present and dictate our future.

To cling to God's promise of strength, let's change our definition of "strength" to align with His. When we experience situations that make us feel weak, we can cling to God's promise to be our strength. Instead of only asking God to take the hard things away, we can also pray, *Lord, have Your way.*

A God We Can Rely On

Complete the chart below by adding your own examples of scriptures that remind us to place our faith in God, as well as scriptures that remind us not to place our faith in the people, places and things of this world. Consider choosing a few of these verses to memorize to help you cling to God's trustworthy promises.

THE BIBLE TEACHES US TO RELY ON THE LORD	THE BIBLE TEACHES US NOT TO RELY ON ...
"... The men of Judah prevailed, because they relied on the LORD, the God of their fathers" (2 Chronicles 13:18).	Human strength: "Woe to those who ... trust in chariots because they are many and in horsemen because they are very strong, but do not look to the Holy One of Israel or consult the LORD!" (Isaiah 31:1)
"Trust in the LORD with all your heart ..." (Proverbs 3:5).	Material things: "He leans against his house, but it does not stand; he lays hold of it, but it does not endure" (Job 8:15).
"Offer right sacrifices, and put your trust in the LORD" (Psalm 4:5).	Human understanding: "... Do not lean on your own understanding" (Proverbs 3:5).
"Those who know your name put their trust in you, for you, O LORD, have not forsaken those who seek you" (Psalm 9:10).	Human works: "For by works of the law no human being will be justified in [God's] sight, since through the law comes knowledge of sin" (Romans 3:20).

DAY 20

EPHESIANS 6:10-20: God will give you His strength so you can stand.

The original audience for today's reading — followers of Jesus in the largely pagan city of Ephesus — needed to be strengthened in resolve. They lived in a world hostile to their beliefs. In response to this need, Paul pointed them (and us!) to God's power.[1]

Ephesians 6:10 reveals both the position of strength ("*be strong **in the Lord***") and the source of strength ("*the strength of **his might***") for the follower of Jesus (emphases added). The verses that follow detail how and why we are to be strong in the Lord.

> To be strong in the Lord, what do we need to put on (Ephesians 6:11)?

According to Ephesians 6:11 and verse 13, why do we need to be strong in the Lord?

There were likely two main influences for the armor of God imagery that Paul wrote about.[2] The first was the Old Testament and its depictions of God as a warrior (e.g., Habakkuk 3:8; Isaiah 42:13; Psalm 35:1-3).

> Isaiah 59:17-18 prophesied that God would appear dressed for war and hand out His judgments. What similarities do you see between Isaiah's prophecy and the armor in Ephesians 6?

With this in mind, we see that the full armor of God isn't just armor *given* by God — it is the *armor of God* Himself, supplied for the Christian. When we put on this armor, we are promised the strength of His might. We will be strong in the Lord, and we will be empowered to stand against the schemes of the devil.

Paul's second influence was the armor of a Roman soldier. Many scholars believe Paul was on house arrest because of his missionary activity when he wrote this letter to the Ephesians, and he may have even been chained to a Roman soldier.[3]

On the day of battle, a Roman soldier's orders were to stand his ground, stand firm and not retreat (similar to Paul's instructions in Ephesians 6:13). As long as each soldier stood his ground, the Roman army was considered to be invincible.[4] And as followers of Jesus, when we individually put on the full armor of God and stand strong in the Lord, we strengthen one another too. This is also why Paul ends the section on the armor of God by telling us to keep alert and persevere in prayer *"for all the saints"* (Ephesians 6:18). Standing firm is not only for us as individuals but for the whole body of Christ.

The schemes of the devil for which we need the full armor of God can sometimes look like separation and alienation. Our enemy knows the strength God provides through community and fellowship with other believers in the Lord.

> Have you ever tried or seen someone else try to be strong in the Lord while remaining separated from other believers in Christ? What was the result?

> How does what you've learned from Ephesians 6 encourage you to connect with other members of the body of Christ?

WEEKEND REFLECTION
WEEK 4

It's hard to disconnect our idea of strength from the feeling of physical fitness and capability — but what we've learned this week has demonstrated that true strength often has little to do with muscle power. It's hard for us to fathom, but Jesus Himself understood what it meant to be strong in the Lord while being physically depleted; when His human body was weak with hunger and thirst (Matthew 4:1-11), and even when He hung on the cross, suffering torture, He still chose righteousness and clung to God's Word.

No, the idea of weakness isn't usually something we celebrate. But here's why that's exciting: If we live long enough, we are sure to experience the pangs of human weakness, yet because of God's promise of strength, weakness in the flesh can still mean strength in the spirit.

It's a math equation that doesn't make sense. Weakness shouldn't equal strength — but in God's economy, it does. This truly is a promise to cling to. And let's not quickly forget what we learned yesterday: We're stronger together. When one of us is weak, together we can share and stand in the strength of the Lord.

PRAYING THE PROMISES (PSALM 96:4-8)
Oh Lord, You are great and greatly to be praised. All other gods are worthless idols, but You, Lord, made the heavens. Splendor and majesty are before You. Strength and beauty are in Your sanctuary. We ascribe to You, Lord, glory and strength! We give You the glory due Your name. In Jesus' name, amen.

NOTES

NOTES

WEEK FIVE

PROMISE OF SECURITY

DAY 21

2 SAMUEL 22: God will be your place of safety.

One definition of "secure" is "to make (a door or container) hard to open; fasten or lock." But in an emotional and spiritual sense, to be secure is to be free — free from fear or doubt, from danger or risk. While we all long for this security, we can probably agree the world is full of danger and risk that in turn causes us to doubt and fear.

The Bible doesn't promise earthly security in the sense that we will never face times of trouble or harm. God does, however, promise us safety and security *in Him* in times of trouble.

The first three verses of today's reading give us many reasons why God is our safe place.

>Record the ways David described God in 2 Samuel 22:2-3.

Each of these titles David ascribed to God was highly personal to him.

>What two-letter word precedes or is included with every description ("*The LORD is
>
>_____ rock and _____ fortress ...*" [v. 2])?

David did not write of God's security because his life had always been free from danger or risk. David knew God as his Rock, Fortress, Refuge and Deliverer precisely because he *needed* a place of safety. He sang of the security found in his Lord because he had experienced the relief of running to God and being saved by Him.

>According to 2 Samuel 22:1 and verses 5-6, what kinds of circumstances had David experienced? (You can also read 1 Samuel 18:8-12 for some background about Saul, Israel's first king, who was **not** a fan of David!)

>What experiences or situations in your life make you feel insecure or unsafe? How can you "*[call] upon the LORD*" in those situations (2 Samuel 22:7)?

As we open our week of study on God's promise of security, we must acknowledge that trials and storms will come. That is not the question. The question is: Where will we turn to find security in the midst of life's storms?

Twice in 2 Samuel 22:2-3, and throughout the entire chapter, David referred to God as his Rock. In the Old Testament, this often served as a symbol for security, parallel to a fortress or a place that would be impossible to capture or destroy.[1]

Jesus also distinguished between building our lives on the Rock of God or on something else. He told His disciples a parable about two builders. One man built his house on rock, and the other built his house on the sand.

> According to Matthew 7:24-27, what happened when both houses encountered rain, floods and winds?

Security begins with God, our Rock, and the decision to build our lives on Him. Second Samuel 22 reminds us of the steadfastness of this God, who ultimately promised to *"build a house for [his] name"* through David's messianic bloodline and to *"establish the throne of his kingdom forever"* (2 Samuel 7:13) — which He has done through Jesus. We build our lives on the Rock of Christ when we hear the words of God and do them (Matthew 7:24; James 1:22). As we do, we will find our place of safety (2 Samuel 22:26-31).

DAY 22

ISAIAH 27:1-6: God will keep watch over you and your future.

It's often easy to tell the difference between land that is well cared for and land that is not. Flower beds that are well kept, for example, appear colorful, healthy and flourishing, while gardens that are not cared for are overcome by weeds.

In today's reading, the prophet Isaiah envisioned God's people as a vineyard, and Isaiah made a promise about this vineyard's security and thriving in the hands of its keeper.

According to Isaiah 27:3, who is the keeper of the vineyard?

How does the keeper care for the vineyard (vv. 3-4)?

Isaiah 27 outlines three specific ways God will keep His vineyard (His people):

1. God will nourish His vineyard. God will water His garden at *"every moment"* (Isaiah 27:3). Later in the book of Isaiah, God described His people as a *"well-watered garden"* (Isaiah 58:11), and Jesus also fulfilled this promise of God when He showed Himself to be Living Water (John 4:14). Whoever drinks from the bottomless well of Jesus' life-giving water will never thirst again.

2. God will guard His vineyard. A typical vineyard in the ancient world was guarded by a wall or hedge and manned at harvest time by a watchman. The watchman's duty was to guard the crop from thieves.[1] God does not trust the care of His vineyard to anyone else but places Himself in the role of watchman *"night and day"* (Isaiah 27:3).

3. God will defend His vineyard. In Isaiah 27:4, the threat of an intruder gives way to a different enemy God defends His vineyard against — *"thorns and briers."* Jesus elaborated on the perils of thorns in Mark 4:1-20, telling a parable in which He described thorns as *"cares of the world and the deceitfulness of riches and the desires for other things,"* which *"choke"* the Word of God in a person's heart and render them unfruitful (Mark 4:19). In Isaiah 27:4-5, the briers could also be said to represent God's enemies — and He offers reconciliation even to them if they will *"make peace with [Him]."*

God's care for His people is consistent, constant and complete, and because of this, His vineyard is safe, healthy and peaceful. Out of the overflow of God's care, His people will take root, blossom and fill the world with fruit (Isaiah 27:6).

The promises in today's reading describe security both for the future and for the present of God's people. We look forward to a future where God will banish Satan (Isaiah 27:1) and dwell among us forever — nourishing and keeping us at every moment. And while we wait, we can count on God's watchful care over us today.

> What does Jesus say in Matthew 6:28-31, and how does this relate to the cultivation imagery in Isaiah 27? What does Jesus promise in Matthew 6:33?

When we thirst for righteousness, we will be filled (Matthew 5:6). When we come to the well of Living Water, we will be satisfied (John 4:13-14).

> How can you let God nourish, guard and defend your heart today so that it is well cared for?

DAY 23

JOHN 15:1-17: God will remain in you.

Yesterday we read about Isaiah's depiction of God's people as a vineyard with God as their keeper. In today's reading, Jesus drew on a similar image to communicate another promise to His disciples.

> In verse 1 of today's reading, Jesus identified Himself and His Father in specific ways. What did Jesus call Himself? What did He call His Father?

In verse 5, Jesus called His disciples *"branches."* This is quite a distinction from what His 12 disciples (all Jewish men) would have assumed themselves to be. Throughout the Old Testament, Israel was identified as a vine or vineyard (Isaiah 5:7; Psalm 80:8). By calling Himself the *"true vine"* (John 15:1), Jesus made a monumental shift in the thinking of His followers and the role of Israel from this point forward.

No longer should God's blessings be understood to flow simply through the nation of ethnic Israel — now they should be understood to flow through Jesus.[1] The way Israel continues to be a blessing to the nations today, just as God prophesied, is through Jesus. And all who respond to Jesus in faith today are the true Israel, *"children of the promise"* (Romans 9:6-8).

Ten times in John 15:4-10, Jesus called His disciples to *"abide"* in Him as the Vine. Abiding conveys the idea of staying in a certain place — not departing or leaving but remaining present. Here, we're called to abide in a close relationship with Jesus, and His call to abide also comes with a promise.

> According to John 15:4-5, when we abide in Christ, what are we promised?

In his letter to the church in Rome, Paul later listed a variety of things that may appear to jeopardize our connection to the love of Christ, including trials, distress, persecution, famine, nakedness, danger and threat of death (Romans 8:35).

However, in spite of all of these things — which Paul had personally experienced and would continue to endure — what did he conclude in Romans 8:39?

This may bring to mind a scene that's common in many adventure movies and books. The main character finds herself hanging precariously on the side of a steep mountain, clinging to the rock and desperately trying to hang on. As her hand begins to slip, she fears she will lose her grip and plummet to her death — but before she falls, a stronger, more stable hand reaches down, grabs her, and holds her safely in his grip. Her grip is not enough to hold on through the trial, but the grip of the one who saves her proves to be all she needs.

> How have you felt like you are trying to hang on in your life? How does it bring you confidence when you know that Jesus hangs on to you?

Our security is ultimately rooted in Christ's finished work on the cross. All those who have placed their trust in Christ are a new creation. As new creatures with new desires, we walk faithfully in the ways of Jesus. And as we abide in Him, Jesus promises He will abide in us. Jesus even notes two ways we can remain or abide in Him: We can ensure His Word remains in us (John 15:7), and we can remain in His love by obeying His commands (v. 10).

Because of Jesus' promise to remain in us, we can rejoice and stand secure. No matter what we face, we are more than conquerors because nothing can separate us from the love of our Savior ... and His love conquers all.

DAY 24
2 PETER 1:1-11: God will give you everything you need.

Our security is often connected with feeling assured in our provision. When we know we have all we need to face the day or the future, we feel secure.

In today's reading, we find that in Christ, we are promised we will always have everything we need.

> This promise is specific though. Second Peter 1:3 promises that God has given us "*all things that pertain to*" what? (Or in the NIV translation, *"everything we need for"* what?)

We are not promised we will have a comfortable life or a safe life. Instead, the Apostle Peter promised that God has given us everything we need for *"life and godliness."*

He also elaborated on why this is so valuable to our security: This promise guards us from the corruption of sinful desire (2 Peter 1:4). Jesus has bestowed on us everything necessary for a life that is growing, healthy and increasing to the full measure of the stature of Christ (Ephesians 4:13).

So what actually is *necessary* for a godly life? Peter's letter doesn't leave us without a path to lead us. In 2 Peter 1:5-7, he employed a literary device called a *sorites*, where one statement builds upon another and ends with a climactic finish.[1]

> What do verses 5-7 say we are to make every effort to do? How are these things similar to or different from what you would typically classify as "necessary" in your life?

> According to verse 8, what will the increasing of these qualities do for us spiritually?

If godliness can be defined as devotion to or fervor for God, the opposite of godliness is the rottenness and corruption of the world. Later in this letter, Peter fleshed out the reality of what happens to those who do not escape this corruption. He described these people as ones who promise each other freedom but are themselves enslaved to sin (2 Peter 2:19).

But when we cooperate with God's promise in 2 Peter 1:3, He ensures us that the godly *"will never fall"* (2 Peter 1:10).

Peter wasn't promising a sinless or untroubled life. Scholars agree this letter was a form of Peter's last words to the Church, likely written in prison while he awaited execution as a martyr for Christ (2 Peter 1:13-14).[2] He desired to teach his audience that the safest way to live may look like suffering for Jesus' sake on earth — but knowing that *"there will be richly provided for you an entrance into the eternal kingdom of our Lord"* (v. 11). In this way, the Bible assures us that godliness holds promise for the present and the future (1 Timothy 4:8).

> How does connecting the promise of security to the pursuit of godliness change your perspective on living securely?

It's probably fair to say we're often devoted to creating a secure life for ourselves or our loved ones. But what if we were most fervently devoted to Jesus, the true source of the security we long for? For the early Christians and for us, we are most secure when we receive and apply the promise that in Christ we *have* everything we need for life and godliness, and we also *will have* everything we need in eternity. No matter what today holds.

DAY 25

HEBREWS 13:1-18: God will never leave you.

The promise of God's presence is like a golden thread woven throughout the Bible. For example: In the Old Testament, God promised to be with Jacob (Abraham's grandson) as he left his family and his homeland (Genesis 28:15). Years later, just before Moses' death, God repeated His promise never to leave the nation of Israel (Deuteronomy 31:6-8). God again gave this promise to Joshua, Moses' successor, as he stood poised to lead Israel into the promised land (Joshua 1:5).

And in today's reading in the New Testament, God repeated His promise to all those who place their faith in Christ.

> Record the promise of Hebrews 13:5 here:

The author of Hebrews bookended this promise with action steps in verses 5-6. The outline looks like this:

1. Call to contentment.
2. Promise that God will never leave us.
3. Reasonable response to the promise.

First, let's look at the life marked by contentment: *"Keep your life free from love of money, and be content with what you have, for he has said, 'I will never leave you nor forsake you'"* (Hebrews 13:5). To be content is to be in a state of peaceful happiness or satisfaction.

> Are you living a contented life today? Why or why not? How does God's presence affect your contentment?

Jesus Himself connected contentment to security when He exhorted His disciples not to worry about their lives but instead to seek first the Kingdom of God and trust His provision (Matthew 6:24-33). Paul also connected contentment to security when he encouraged a fellow believer named Timothy that *"godliness with contentment is great gain"* (1 Timothy 6:6).

The call to contentment shifts our focus from what we think we need to be secure to the sufficiency of Jesus. We learned yesterday that in Jesus, we have everything we need (2 Peter 1:3). We are secure because Jesus is sufficient, and He will never leave us.

> Hebrews 13:11 alludes to how God's people used to make continual animal sacrifices and offerings to seek forgiveness and security in their relationship with God. What does verse 12 say Jesus did *"in order to sanctify"* us today? What did He secure forever? (See verse 14!)

Let's also read Hebrews 13:5 in the Amplified Bible translation. It says:

"He has said, 'I WILL NEVER [under any circumstances] DESERT YOU [nor give you up nor leave you without support, nor will I in any degree leave you helpless], NOR WILL I FORSAKE or LET YOU DOWN or RELAX MY HOLD ON YOU [assuredly not]!'"

> How does this deepen your understanding of the vastness of God's promise? Write down the words that stand out to you and why they mean so much to you.

> According to Hebrews 13:6, what is our reasonable response to such a promise?

Because of God's promise never to desert us, leave us helpless or let us down, we can confidently say, "I am not afraid!"

God fulfilled His promise to Jacob (Genesis 31:3; Genesis 31:17-18; Genesis 33:18-20).

He fulfilled His promise to Moses, the nation of Israel, and Joshua (Joshua 21:43-45).

And we can confidently trust Him to fulfill His promise to us: *"Behold, I am with you always, to the end of the age"* (Matthew 28:20).

WEEKEND REFLECTION
WEEK 5

Our quest for security often prompts us to do more — more fixing and arranging of what we think we can control to try to orchestrate a scenario free from danger, risk or harm. But our doing always leads back to the same place: exhaustion, confusion and running out of options.

We pray this week has given you a better place to find security than what you can arrange on your own. As we conclude our study on God's promise of security in Him, let's try a simple but powerful way to spend time with Jesus: It involves quieting ourselves and being still.

If you're someone who loves to stay busy, you might feel like this is not for you, disliking the idea of stillness because it feels futile and unproductive. But can we encourage you, friend? As you sit still, God will meet you in this quiet time with Him.

Before you move to the prayer below, take a few minutes and be still with God. Silence the noises around you, and do your best to quiet your thoughts. Then let God's promises fill your heart and mind.

PRAYING THE PROMISES (PSALM 91)
Dear God, today I choose to abide in the shelter of the Most High and find rest in the shadow of the Almighty. You are my refuge and my place of safety. You are my God, and I trust in You. May Your promises be my armor and protection. Rescue and protect me today. Let no evil conquer me, and answer me when I call. Be with me in times of trouble. In Jesus' name, amen.

NOTES

NOTES

CLINGING TO THE PROMISES WHEN YOU ARE AFRAID

Dear God, today I am facing these fears in my life:

To cling to Your promises, I will remember Your Word says:

"What then shall we say to these things? If God is for us, who can be against us?" *(Romans 8:31).*

"The Lord is on my side; I will not fear. What can man do to me?" *(Psalm 118:6).*

"Don't worry about anything; instead, pray about everything. Tell God what you need, and thank him for all he has done" *(Philippians 4:6, NLT).*

"Therefore do not be anxious about tomorrow, for tomorrow will be anxious for itself. Sufficient for the day is its own trouble" *(Matthew 6:34).*

"Give all your worries and cares to God, for he cares about you" *(1 Peter 5:7, NLT).*

In Jesus' name, amen.

WEEK SIX

PROMISE OF HOPE

DAY 26

HEBREWS 10:19-39: God will be faithful.

Biblical hope is tied directly to our confidence in the God whose promises cannot fail. Today's Scripture reading paves the way for how we can let hope guide our thoughts and actions.

Hebrews 10:19-39 serves as a summary of all that the writer of Hebrews said up to this point in the book. We have confidence in Jesus because of what He accomplished on the cross and because of His role as our great High Priest (Hebrews 10:19-21).

Because we have hope in Jesus, Hebrews directs Christians toward three action steps:

1. Draw near to God (Hebrews 10:22).
2. Hold fast the confession of our hope (Hebrews 10:23).
3. Stir up one another to love and good works (Hebrews 10:24).

   According to verse 23, what reason do we have for holding fast the confession of our hope?

Hebrews 10:32-36 details what it looks like to hold fast to the confession of our hope — but first, verses 26-31 show the opposite. The consequences of *"sinning deliberately after receiving the knowledge of the truth"* (v. 26) encourage us not only to hold fast to Jesus but to hold fast without wavering.

PRIESTHOOD IN THE SCRIPTURES

To help us understand Jesus as our High Priest, here are a few key terms in Hebrews 10 we need to understand:

"Holy places" (v. 19) in the ancient Jewish temple were places where only priests could enter God's presence (1 Chronicles 6:49; Leviticus 16:17). In Christ, all believers enjoy God's presence!

"The curtain" (v. 20) refers to the veil that set apart the Most Holy Place of the temple (Exodus 26:33-34). This veil was torn when Jesus died on the cross, granting open access to God through faith in Him (Matthew 27:51).

"Great priest" (v. 21) shows that Jesus is better than any other priest in history because His self-sacrifice on our behalf is perfect and effective forever (Leviticus 21:10-15; Hebrews 5:1-4).

What can the person who does not hold fast to hope in Christ expect (Hebrews 10:26-31)?

What is in store for the one who holds fast to hope in Christ (Hebrews 10:35-36)?

Christians in the early Church were publicly reproached, persecuted and robbed (vv. 33-34) — which may have left some thinking, *Maybe we've overcommitted to this whole "Jesus" thing. Should we really risk our lives for Him? Should we even keep going to church?* Scholars point out that one reason the author of Hebrews wrote this passage was because he believed his original audience was in danger of relaxing their hold on the hope they had in Jesus.[1] We, too, can heed this warning.

Of the three action steps presented in Hebrews 10, which one could you be more aware of or practice more?

What is one thing you will do today to hold tightly to the hope you have in Jesus and put into practice the action you wrote about in your answer above?

Today's reading concludes with a reminder of the promise we hope in.

Read Hebrews 10:35-36 and fill in the blanks below:

"Therefore do not throw away your _____ , which has a great _____ . For you have need of _____ , so that when you have done the _____ of _____ you may receive what is _____ ."

Our author bookended this passage with the confident assurance we have in Jesus (v. 1) and the call to hold tightly to our hope in Him (v. 36). The Greek verb translated *"you may receive"* in verse 36 implies not merely obtaining the promise but carrying it away to be used and enjoyed.[2]

This brings to mind where we began our study. The promises of God are not merely like a gift under the Christmas tree that we look at and point to — they are meant to be unwrapped, opened, received and enjoyed.

DAY 27
ROMANS 8:18-30: God will work all things for good.

Today's reading is full of hope — literally. Five times in Romans 8:24-25, Paul used the word *"hope"*! These two verses teach us a few things about hope:

1. In hope we were saved (Romans 8:24).
2. Hope is not seen (Romans 8:24).
3. Hope requires us to wait with patience (Romans 8:25).

With these three things in mind, let's break down the main promise we'll focus on today.

> What promise does Romans 8:28 record?

This verse begins with the hope in which we were saved as it distinguishes who the promise is for: *"those who love God."* The Amplified Bible builds out what is promised here. It says:

"And we know [with great confidence] that God [who is deeply concerned about us] causes all things to work together [as a plan] for good for those who love God, to those who are called according to His plan and purpose" (Romans 8:28).

Coupled with God's deep concern for His people, we are assured that God causes all things to work together for good for those who love Him.

This brings us to the part of hope that is not seen. Many times God's work is not immediately visible to us.

> Consider a hard situation or relationship in your life where you do not see anything good happening right now. How does Romans 8:28 give you hope for that situation?

How does the idea of unseen hope help us cling to other invisible blessings promised in today's reading? For instance, how do we trust that the Holy Spirit is praying for us even though we can't see Him (v. 26)? How do we look forward to *"glory that is to be revealed"* (v. 18)?

Finally, as we consider the plans and purposes God is working out, we're reminded that hope requires patience. The good He works out according to His ongoing and eternal plan often requires us to wait.

According to Romans 8:23, even as we suffer, how can we wait? What are we waiting for?

The Old Testament gives us an example of the Romans 8:28 promise as it played out in the life of Joseph. Joseph, one of the sons of Israel, was sold by his brothers into slavery (Genesis 37). But in the midst of Joseph's suffering, twice the Bible tells us the Lord was with him (Genesis 39:2; Genesis 39:21). Through many trials and troubles, God brought Joseph to a position of leadership in Egypt (Genesis 41:37-45).

After many years, he reunited with his brothers, and God positioned him to save them from famine and death. At that time Joseph realized: *"As for you, you meant evil against me, but God meant it for good, to bring it about that many people should be kept alive, as they are today"* (Genesis 50:20).

Joseph's life was not absent of suffering, but it also was not absent of God's good, perfect and pleasing will.

How does knowing that our hope is unseen give you confidence to trust God is at work in your circumstances today?

TIMELINE OF
JOSEPH'S LIFE

GENESIS 30:22-24 — Rachel gave birth to Joseph

GENESIS 37:5-11 — Joseph had dreams about his family

GENESIS 37:12-27 — Joseph's brothers sold him into slavery

GENESIS 39:2-6 — Joseph became overseer in Potiphar's house

GENESIS 44:1-13 — Joseph tested his brothers

GENESIS 45:1-15 — Joseph revealed his identity to his brothers

GENESIS 45:25-47:12 — Jacob moved his family to Egypt

GENESIS 47:13-50:26 — Jacob and his sons settled and remained in Egypt

GENESIS 39:7-18

Joseph was imprisoned

GENESIS 39:21-23

Joseph interpreted prisoners' dreams, and his interpretations came true

GENESIS 39:19-20

Joseph resisted Potiphar's wife, and she accused him

GENESIS 40:1-23

Joseph became overseer of the prison

Joseph's brothers came to Egypt to buy grain

Pharaoh promoted Joseph

GENESIS 41:46-57

GENESIS 41:14-36

GENESIS 42:1-17

GENESIS 41:37-45

Joseph prepared for famine

Joseph interpreted Pharaoh's dreams

DAY 28

MATTHEW 11:25-30: God will give you rest when you are weary and burdened.

When the burdens of life weigh heavily on our shoulders, hope can feel unattainable. At times, it may feel like no one is coming to help, and we may wonder how much longer we can carry the load alone ...

In today's reading, Jesus offers us the solution to this problem.

> According to Matthew 11:28, what two groups of people does Jesus call to come to Him?

Some scholars suggest Jesus was referring to two kinds of loads: The Greek word He used for *"labor"* points to the kind of load we place on ourselves, like the self-reliance we talked about in Week 4 of our study. The word for *"heavy laden,"* however, points to loads placed on us by others.[1] The people in Jesus' original audience may have associated this with the burden of the mandates placed on them by the religious leaders of their day.[2]

But for those who come to Him, Jesus promises rest.

> How do you define "rest"? What would it look like for you to have *"rest for your soul"* (v. 29)?

Interestingly, Jesus' promise of rest invites us to *"take [His] yoke"* (v. 29). A yoke is a wooden bar placed around the necks of two or more animals so that they can work effectively together. In ancient times, yokes would have been tailor-made to fit so that they didn't choke or hurt the animals as they worked. A yoke was also often used to tie a younger, weaker animal together with an older, stronger one so that the stronger animal could carry the load while the weaker one learned.[3]

Jesus' yoke is not one that relinquishes us from all responsibility; instead, it brings us into His rest that comes from a mind and soul at ease. When we come to Jesus, we can expect a yoke that is easy, well fitting and light.

How does Jesus' promise of an easy yoke and light burden remove the weight of restlessness and exhaustion from you today?

How is being yoked to Jesus different from being yoked to other things (your job, your kids, your spouse, your finances, etc.)? To read about other "yokes" in Scripture, see Lamentations 1:14, Psalm 106:28 and Galatians 5:1.

You may have already identified this as a promise that requires our participation. ● The hope of rest we have in Jesus begins with His gracious call and our response to His invitation: *"Come to me, all who labor and are heavy laden ..."* (Matthew 11:28).

Come — the same word Jesus used when He called His disciples (Matthew 4:19, NIV).
Come — the same word Jesus used in the parable of the wedding feast, inviting others to join Him (Matthew 22:4).
Come — the same word Jesus used when He told about the day we will stand before God and He will invite us into eternal glory (Matthew 25:34).

Today, just as we did when we first believed, let's accept Jesus' invitation to come to Him and cling to the hope of His promise of rest.

DAY 29

JOHN 11:17-44: God will raise you up when life feels hopeless.

Before we dive into today's reading, let's set the stage: In the opening verses of John 11, Jesus received word that His friend Lazarus was ill. Lazarus' sisters sent Him the message (vv. 1-3). Upon receiving the news, Jesus stayed where He was for two more days, then traveled to the village of Bethany, where Lazarus and his sisters lived (vv. 6-11).

In the first verse of today's reading, we find a significant detail concerning the events that followed.

> According to John 11:17, how many days had Lazarus been in the tomb when Jesus arrived?

The general belief in ancient Jewish culture was that the spirit of a deceased person would hover over the body for three days in anticipation of a possible return into the body. But on the third day, it was believed that the body lost its color and the spirit was "locked out." Therefore, the passing of the third day signaled that all hope of life was lost.[1]

> Describe a time when you have felt like all hope was lost. Have you ever felt like Jesus showed up too late to help you?

Lazarus' sisters had probably hoped Jesus would come and heal Lazarus while he was alive. Four days after Lazarus died, Martha and Mary's words expressed hopelessness and disappointment (John 11:21; John 11:32).

> How did Jesus answer Martha in verses 23-26? What promise did He make about *"whoever believes in me"*?

While Martha confirmed her belief that her brother would rise again *"on the last day"* (v. 24), scholars agree she was not expecting Jesus to restore Lazarus to life right away.[2] This was evident when Jesus called for the stone covering Lazarus' tomb to be taken away: Instead of eagerly obliging, Martha cautioned Jesus about the reality of the dead body inside (v. 39).

> According to verse 40, how did Jesus answer Martha this time?

Jesus encouraged Martha not to look at the hopelessness of the situation but reminded her of what He had promised moments before: *"I am the resurrection and the life ..."* (v. 25).

And Jesus' resurrection of Lazarus also foreshadows the eternal resurrection of all those who believe in Jesus (1 Corinthians 15:21-23). The promise that we will be raised up on the last day holds hope for our future — and it also holds hope for today. Because Jesus is the resurrection and the life, He calls us out of the spiritual grave of our sin and shame today.

> When Jesus called Lazarus out of his grave, He issued a command. What did Jesus tell the people to do in John 11:44?

Because of Jesus' promise to raise us up, we are no longer dead in our sins and slaves to the ways of flesh. The resurrection life Jesus promises begins immediately when we believe in Him. And in the same way Lazarus needed to put off his grave clothes, when we follow Jesus, we, too, need to put off our old selves and put on new selves (Ephesians 4:20-24).

When our circumstances feel hopeless, we, like Martha, can turn our eyes away from the hopelessness of our situation and remember Jesus' promise.

DAY 30
REVELATION 21:1-8: God will wipe away every tear.

As we close our study on the promises of God, there's perhaps no better passage to reflect on than Revelation 21:1-8. This promise is found in the last book of the Bible, which is dedicated to prophecies (aka promises!) that God revealed to the Apostle John in relation to eternity.

These verses detail the day when our hope in Christ, which is already real and powerful today, will be fully and eternally realized as we join Jesus in His heavenly Kingdom. Almost every verse of Revelation 21 gives us a promise from our faithful God.

> Write out today's passage in the space below. (Yes, it will take some time — but it's worth it!) As you write, meditate on any phrases God brings to your attention, and ask Him to give you an increasing appreciation for His living and active Word.

Let's do some hands-on study of the text together. If you have different colored pens or highlighters, you may want to use those. You can do the following exercises right here in your study guide or directly in your Bible, if you'd prefer.

Underline the promises that follow the words *"He will," "they will"* and *"God himself will"* in verses 3-4. What does God promise will be no more?

Circle the promises that follow the words *"I am," "I will"* and *"he will"* in verses 5-7. How do these promises relate to some of the promises we have already studied together? (For instance, look back at God's promise of Living Water from Day 22 and His promises of new identity from Day 16.)

God promises a heavenly heritage to *"the one who conquers"* (Revelation 21:7). Does that promise include you and me? Let's consider …

On Day 23 of our study, we learned that when we believe in Jesus and follow Him, nothing can separate us from His love (Romans 8:35-39). In Romans 8:37, Paul says those who follow Christ are *"more than"* what?

The Apostle John also wrote about those who "conquer," or "overcome," in his letters. Look up the verses below and record what they say about overcomers:

1 JOHN 4:4:

1 JOHN 5:4-5:

Finally, on Day 3, we learned that in the world we will have trials and trouble, but Jesus gives us His peace. Why does Jesus say we can *"take heart"* (John 16:33)?

Friend, some days, we find ourselves weeping in this broken world ... but one day our tears will be *"former things"* (Revelation 21:4). God's declaration *"It is done!"* in verse 6 is plural in the original Greek and points to all that has to occur to usher in God's final victory. It is meant as reassurance to the Christian that God is in command and that all things will work out just as He intends.[1] Because God will bring His redemptive work to completion, we have hope for today and forever. Because He is faithful, we can endure faithfully to the end.

As we close our study together, let us encourage you, sister: Your King is coming soon, and His reward is with Him (Revelation 22:12).

WEEKEND REFLECTION
WEEK 6

Though this week marks the end of our study together, the promises we've looked at in this guide represent only the beginning of all God's promises in Scripture. We couldn't possibly cover them all in just six weeks. This truly is the tip of the iceberg — and that's a beautiful thing!

We pray this study has only increased your hunger to know God and His promises more deeply and to cling to God and His Word more often. God's timeless promises to us are true throughout all generations. As we cling to God's promise of hope for our present and our future, we can also be examples to the generation that follows us and pass on God's great and precious promises for them to cling to.

It's been a blessing to journey with you through this study. We pray you'll keep it close and come back to it often. The more you pray God's promises, remember God's promises and cling to God's promises, you will see it is possible to keep holding on — because the God you're holding on to will never let you go.

PRAYING THE PROMISES (PSALM 71)
Dear God, I ask that You would turn Your ear to listen to me and set me free. O Lord, You alone are my hope. I come to You for protection and rescue. I will keep holding on to You and hoping in Your help. I will praise You more and more. I will tell everyone about Your righteousness. In Jesus' name, amen.

NOTES

NOTES

NOTES

NOTES

NOTES

NOTES

NOTES

NOTES

ENDNOTES

WHAT ARE THE PROMISES OF GOD?

[1] Watson, Richard. "Promise." *A Biblical and Theological Dictionary*, New York, NY: Lane & Scott, 1851, p. 781.

PROMISES OF GOD IN THE OLD TESTAMENT AND THE NEW TESTAMENT

[1] Walker, W. L. "Promise." *The International Standard Bible Encyclopaedia*, ed. James Orr et al. Chicago, IL: The Howard-Severance Company, 1915, p. 2459.

[2] Elwell, Walter A. and Philip Wesley Comfort. *Tyndale Bible Dictionary*, Tyndale Reference Library, Wheaton, IL: Tyndale House Publishers, 2001, p. 323.

[3] Elwell, Walter A. and Philip Wesley Comfort. *Tyndale Bible Dictionary*, Tyndale Reference Library, Wheaton, IL: Tyndale House Publishers, 2001, p. 323.

[4] Elwell, Walter A. and Philip Wesley Comfort. *Tyndale Bible Dictionary*, Tyndale Reference Library, Wheaton, IL: Tyndale House Publishers, 2001, pp. 1080-1081.

HOW DO I KNOW WHICH OF GOD'S PROMISES ARE FOR ME?

[1] John Piper. "Does Proverbs Promise My Child Will Not Stray?" *Desiring God*, August 20, 2015. https://www.desiringgod.org/interviews/does-proverbs-promise-my-child-will-not-stray.

WEEK 1: PROMISE OF PEACE

DAY 1

[1] Elwell, Walter A. and Philip Wesley Comfort. *Tyndale Bible Dictionary*, Tyndale Reference Library, Wheaton, IL: Tyndale House Publishers, 2001, pp. 1303-1304.

DAY 2

[1] Matthews, Victor Harold, Mark W. Chavalas, and John H. Walton. "Isaiah 9:4." *The IVP Bible Background Commentary: Old Testament*, Downers Grove, IL: InterVarsity Press, 2000.

[2] Matthews, Victor Harold, Mark W. Chavalas, and John H. Walton. "Isaiah 9:5-10." *The IVP Bible Background Commentary: Old Testament*, Downers Grove, IL: InterVarsity Press, 2000.

[3] Motyer, Alec J. *Isaiah: An Introduction and Commentary*, vol. 20. Tyndale Old Testament Commentaries, Downers Grove, IL: InterVarsity Press, 1999, p. 102.

BIBLICAL WORD STUDY: "PEACE"

[1] "šālôm - Strong's Hebrew Lexicon (ESV)." Blue Letter Bible. https://www.blueletterbible.org/lexicon/h7965/esv/wlc/0-1/.

[2] "eirēnē - Strong's Greek Lexicon (ESV)." Blue Letter Bible. https://www.blueletterbible.org/lexicon/g1515/esv/mgnt/0-1/.

DAY 3

[1] Carson, D. A. *The Gospel according to John*. The Pillar New Testament Commentary, Leicester, England; Grand Rapids, MI: InterVarsity Press; W.B. Eerdmans, 1991, pp. 505-506.

DAY 4

[1] Motyer, Alec J. *Isaiah: An Introduction and Commentary*, vol. 20. Tyndale Old Testament Commentaries, Downers Grove, IL: InterVarsity Press, 1999, p. 195.

[2] "Amplified Bible Info." Lockman Foundation, https://www.lockman.org/amplified-bible-amp/.

[3] Motyer, Alec J. *Isaiah: An Introduction and Commentary*, vol. 20. Tyndale Old Testament Commentaries, Downers Grove, IL: InterVarsity Press, 1999, p. 198.

DAY 5

[1] Vincent, Marvin Richardson. *Word Studies in the New Testament*, vol. 3. New York: Charles Scribner's Sons, 1887, p. 458.

[2] Hansen, G. Walter. *The Letter to the Philippians*. The Pillar New Testament Commentary, Grand Rapids, MI; Nottingham, England: William B. Eerdmans Publishing Company, 2009, pp. 290-291.

[3] Hansen, G. Walter. *The Letter to the Philippians*. The Pillar New Testament Commentary, Grand Rapids, MI; Nottingham, England: William B. Eerdmans Publishing Company, 2009, pp. 290-291.

WEEK 2: PROMISE OF GUIDANCE

DAY 6

[1] Kidner, Derek. *Genesis: An Introduction and Commentary*, vol. 1. Tyndale Old Testament Commentaries, Downers Grove, IL: InterVarsity Press, 1967, pp. 125-126.

DAY 8

[1] Borchert, Gerald L. *John 12-21*, vol. 25B, The New American Commentary, Nashville: Broadman & Holman Publishers, 2002, p. 165.

DAY 10

[1] Evans, Tony. *The Power of Knowing God*. Harvest House Publishers, 2020.

[2] "*haplōs* - Strong's Greek Lexicon (ESV)." Blue Letter Bible. https://www.blueletterbible.org/lexicon/g574/esv/mgnt/0-1/.

[3] Moo, Douglas J. *James: An Introduction and Commentary*, ed. Eckhard J. Schnabel, second edition., vol. 16. Tyndale New Testament Commentaries, Nottingham, England: InterVarsity Press, 2015, pp. 85-86.

[4] Moo, Douglas J. *The Letter of James*. The Pillar New Testament Commentary, Grand Rapids, MI; Leicester, England: Eerdmans; Apollos, 2000, p. 60.

WEEK 3: PROMISE OF COMFORT

DAY 11

[1] Matthews, Victor Harold, Mark W. Chavalas, and John H. Walton. "Genesis 16:13." *The IVP Bible Background Commentary: Old Testament*, Downers Grove, IL: InterVarsity Press, 2000.

[2] Mathews, K. A. *Genesis 11:27-50:26*, vol. 1B. The New American Commentary, Nashville: Broadman & Holman Publishers, 2005, p. 191.

[3] Larsen, Kevin W. "El Roi." *The Lexham Bible Dictionary*, ed. John D. Barry et al., Bellingham, WA: Lexham Press, 2016.

DAY 12

[1] Block, Daniel Isaac. *The Book of Ezekiel, Chapters 25-48*. The New International Commentary on the Old Testament, Grand Rapids, MI: Wm. B. Eerdmans Publishing Co., 1997, p. 289.

DAY 13

[1] Carson, D. A. *The Gospel according to John*. The Pillar New Testament Commentary, Leicester, England; Grand Rapids, MI: InterVarsity Press; W.B. Eerdmans, 1991, pp. 382-383.

WEEK 4: PROMISE OF STRENGTH

DAY 16

[1] Waltke, Bruce K. and Cathi J. Fredricks, *Genesis: A Commentary*. Grand Rapids, MI: Zondervan, 2001, pp. 258-259.

[2] Matthews, Victor Harold, Mark W. Chavalas, and John H. Walton. "Genesis 17:1-8." *The IVP Bible Background Commentary: Old Testament*, Downers Grove, IL: InterVarsity Press, 2000.

[3] Waltke, Bruce K. and Cathi J. Fredricks, *Genesis: A Commentary*. Grand Rapids, MI: Zondervan, 2001, pp. 259-260.

DAY 17

[1] Oswalt, John N. *The Book of Isaiah, Chapters 40-66*. The New International Commentary on the Old Testament, Grand Rapids, MI: Wm. B. Eerdmans Publishing Co., 1998, pp. 85-86.

[2] Oswalt, John N. *The Book of Isaiah, Chapters 40-66*. The New International Commentary on the Old Testament, Grand Rapids, MI: Wm. B. Eerdmans Publishing Co., 1998, p. 92.

DAY 20

[1] Lincoln, Andrew T. *Ephesians*, vol. 42. Word Biblical Commentary, Dallas: Word, Incorporated, 1990, pp. 440-441.

[2] Keener, Craig S. "Ephesians 6:10-20." *The IVP Bible Background Commentary: New Testament*. Downers Grove, IL: InterVarsity Press, 1993.

[3] Stott, John R. W. *The Message of Ephesians*. Downers Grove, IL: InterVarsity Press, 1979, p. 276.

[4] Keener, Craig S. "Ephesians 6:10-11." *The IVP Bible Background Commentary: New Testament*, Downers Grove, IL: InterVarsity Press, 1993.

WEEK 5: PROMISE OF SECURITY

DAY 21

[1] Matthews, Victor Harold, Mark W. Chavalas, and John H. Walton. "2 Samuel 22:2-3." *The IVP Bible Background Commentary: Old Testament*, Downers Grove, IL: InterVarsity Press, 2000.

DAY 22

[1] Elwell, Walter A. and Philip Wesley Comfort. *Tyndale Bible Dictionary*. Tyndale Reference Library, Wheaton, IL: Tyndale House Publishers, 2001, p. 1286.

DAY 23

[1] Köstenberger, Andreas J. "John." *Commentary on the New Testament Use of the Old Testament*. Grand

Rapids, MI; Nottingham, UK: Baker Academic; Apollos, 2007, p. 491.

DAY 24

[1] Bauckham, Richard J. *2 Peter, Jude*, vol. 50. Word Biblical Commentary, Dallas: Word, Incorporated, 1983, p. 192.

[2] Bauckham, Richard J. *2 Peter, Jude*, vol. 50. Word Biblical Commentary, Dallas: Word, Incorporated, 1983, p. 176.

WEEK 6: PROMISE OF HOPE

DAY 26

[1] Guthrie, Donald. *Hebrews: An Introduction and Commentary*, vol. 15. Tyndale New Testament Commentaries, Downers Grove, IL: InterVarsity Press, 1983, pp. 216-217.

[2] Vincent, Marvin Richardson. *Word Studies in the New Testament*, vol. 4, New York, NY: Charles Scribner's Sons, 1887, p. 508.

DAY 28

[1] Guzik, David. "Matthew 11—Not the Messiah They Expected Him to Be." *Enduring Word Bible Commentary*, 2018, https://enduringword.com/bible-commentary/matthew-11.

[2] France, R. T. *The Gospel according to Matthew: An Introduction and Commentary*. Grand Rapids, MI: Eerdmans, 1985, p. 200.

[3] Barclay, William. *Gospel of Matthew*. Louisville, KY: Westminster John Knox, 2001, pp. 20-21.

DAY 29

[1] Borchert, Gerald L. *John 1-11*, vol. 25A. The New American Commentary, Nashville: Broadman & Holman Publishers, 1996, p. 354.

[2] Kruse, Colin G. *John: An Introduction and Commentary*, ed. Eckhard J. Schnabel, second edition., vol. 4. Tyndale New Testament Commentaries, London: InterVarsity Press, 2017, pp. 288-289.

DAY 30

[1] Morris, Leon. *Revelation: An Introduction and Commentary*, vol. 20. Tyndale New Testament Commentaries, Downers Grove, IL: InterVarsity Press, 1987, pp. 234-235.

ABOUT
PROVERBS 31 MINISTRIES

She is clothed with strength and dignity;
she can laugh at the days to come.

PROVERBS 31:25

Proverbs 31 Ministries is a nondenominational, nonprofit Christian ministry that seeks to lead women into a personal relationship with Christ. With Proverbs 31:10-31 as a guide, Proverbs 31 Ministries reaches women in the middle of their busy days through free devotions, podcast episodes, speaking events, conferences, resources, and training in the call to write, speak and lead others.

We are real women offering real-life solutions to those striving to maintain life's balance, in spite of today's hectic pace and cultural pull away from godly principles.

Wherever a woman may be on her spiritual journey, Proverbs 31 Ministries exists to be a trusted friend who understands the challenges she faces and walks by her side, encouraging her as she walks toward the heart of God.

Visit us online today at proverbs31.org!

P31
PROVERBS 31
ministries

OUR NEXT STUDY IS COMING SOON ...

Can I Be Honest? How To Process and Express Your Emotions in a Biblical Way

A STUDY OF THE BOOK OF LAMENTATIONS

AVAILABLE FEBRUARY 2024
AT P31BOOKSTORE.COM